How to Do "The Three Bears" with Two Hands

PERFORMING WITH PUPPETS

Walter Minkel

AMERICAN LIBRARY ASSOCIATION
Chicago and London
2000

Project manager: Joan A. Grygel

Cover design: Lesiak Design

Text design: Dianne M. Rooney

Composition in Berkeley and Univers using TeX 3.14 by BookComp, Inc.

Printed on 50-pound white offset, a pH-neutral stock, and bound in 10-point coated cover stock by McNaughton & Gunn

While extensive effort has gone into ensuring the reliability of information appearing in this book, the publisher makes no warranty, express or implied, on the accuracy or reliability of the information, and does not assume and hereby disclaims any liability to any person for any loss or damage caused by errors or omissions in this publication.

The paper used in this publication meets the minimum requirements of American National Standard for Information Sciences—Permanence of Paper for Printed Library Materials, ANSI Z39.48–1992. ♾

Library of Congress Cataloging-in-Publication Data

Minkel, Walter.
    How to do "The three bears" with two hands : performing with
puppets / by Walter Minkel.
        p. cm.
    Includes bibliographical references and index.
    ISBN 0-8389-0756-3
    1. Puppet theater.   2. Libraries and puppets.   3. Puppet theater
in education.   I. Title.
PN1972.M55   1999
791.5'3–dc21   99-28228

Printed in the United States of America.

04 03 02 01 00   5 4 3 2 1

CONTENTS

FIGURES   *v*

INTRODUCTION   *1*

1   Why Puppetry in the Library?   *4*

Is Puppetry for You?   *6*
What Is Puppetry?   *7*
Communication through Puppets   *8*
Four Kinds of Puppets   *10*
Puppetry as Art   *12*

2   Developing Technique   *14*

The Performer's Attitude   *14*
Creating Your Characters   *16*
Breath Control and Voice   *17*
Manipulation—A Puppet's Body Language   *20*
Entrances and Exits   *26*

3   Script Writing and Adaptation   *27*

Elements of a Good Script   *28*
Original or Adaptation?   *30*
Adaptation and Copyright   *30*
Sensitivity Issues and Classic Tales   *35*

4   The One-Person Puppet Program   *41*

The Puppet Mascot   *42*
Storytelling with Puppets and Props   *46*
Three Bears with Two Hands   *48*
Staging Your Solo Show   *50*
Working with Another Puppeteer   *54*

5 Puppets, Stages, Scenery, and Props 55

Puppets *55*
Stages and "Nonstages" *60*
Simple Scenery and Props *65*

6 Puppetry as Part of Your Job 68

Know Your Audience *68*
Performing in a Library *69*
Sample Program Activities *74*
Performing Outside the Library *76*

APPENDIXES

A Five Puppet Show Scripts *79*

The Three Little Pigs *80*
The Three Billy Goats Gruff *92*
Who's the Squonk? *100*
Coyote and the Galloping Rock *104*
The Magic Knapsack *118*

B Stage-Building Plans *130*

Closed Proscenium Stretched-Cloth Stage *130*
Open Proscenium PVC Pipe Stage *140*

C Sources and Resources *149*

INDEX *153*

FIGURES

2.1   Dimensions of the Human Voice   19
2.2   Correct Eye Contact with Speaker   22
2.3   Incorrect Eye Contact   22
2.4   Mouth Puppet Hand Position in Natural and Trained Positions   23
2.5   Glove Puppet Arms in Natural and Trained Positions   24
2.6   Anatomy of a Glove Puppet   24
2.7   Mouth Puppet Speech Movement   25

4.1   Stick Puppet Example   47
4.2   Stick Puppets with Different Facial Expressions on Reverse Sides   48

5.1   Standard and Enhanced Eyes for Puppets   57
5.2   Puppet Characters in Proportion to Each Other   59
5.3   Hand-and-Rod Puppet Example   60
5.4   Three Basic Designs for Puppet Stages   61
5.5   Parts of a Closed Proscenium Puppet Stage   62
5.6   Prop Holders inside the Stage   64
5.7   Dowel Peg Scenery Holder   66

6.1   Puppeteer-Only Performance Zone   72

A.1   Houses for "The Three Little Pigs"   91
A.2   Bridge for "The Three Billy Goats Gruff"   99
A.3   Scenery and Props for "Who's the Squonk?"   104
A.4   Some Characters for "Coyote and the Galloping Rock"   118
A.5   Scenery and Props for "The Magic Knapsack"   128

B.1   Sections for a Closed Proscenium Stretched-Cloth Stage   132
B.2   Section of Stretched-Cloth Stage with Top and Bottom Stretched and
        Stapled   133
B.3   The Proper Height for the Proscenium Section   134
B.4   Hinge Straps for Sections 4, 5, and 6 of a Stretched-Cloth Stage   135
B.5   Holes and Dowels to Join the Top and Bottom Halves of a Stretched-
        Cloth Stage   136
B.6   Fold-Down Prop Shelf for a Stretched-Cloth Stage   136
B.7   Playboard for a Stretched-Cloth Stage   137
B.8   Side and Overhead Views of Curtains and Puppeteer Position   138
B.9   Lighting Configuration for a Stretched-Cloth Stage   139

B.10 Method for Keeping Puppets Ready for Use   139
B.11 Tote Bag for a Stretched-Cloth Stage   140
B.12 Diagram of a PVC Pipe Open Proscenium Stage   143
B.13 Sections of a Permanently Glued PVC Pipe Stage   144
B.14 Prop Shelf for a PVC Pipe Stage   144
B.15 Playboard Assembly for a PVC Pipe Stage   145
B.16 Layout of Cloth and Velcro for a PVC Pipe Stage   146
B.17 Lighting Configurations for a PVC Pipe Stage   148

INTRODUCTION

We performers know how to draw an audience in. I entitled this book *How to Do "The Three Bears" with Two Hands,* but—abracadabra-change-o—I have no intention of showing you how to do that. Sorry, I actually don't recommend doing "Goldilocks and the Three Bears" as a one-person show; I tried it once and it doesn't work very well. Instead, having lured your interest with the title (and a promise that I *will* show you how to perform "The Three Little Pigs" and "The Three Billy Goats Gruff"), let me now show you some of the more prosaic—but very useful—elements of being a puppeteer in a school or public library.

Puppetry in this book is not presented as a class project or an educational tool or as an instrument of "good and noble cause" propaganda spreading, but as a performing art. This art can be awe-inspiring in the hands of a professional master puppeteer, but it can also be "pretty good" in our hands—the hands of library and media center staff people. Through *How to Do "The Three Bears" with Two Hands* you will learn how to develop the talents you have, become a better performer, and move an audience of children.

There are plenty of "how to give a puppet show" books available with scripts of specific plays and plenty of books that tell you how to make puppets out of socks and egg cartons. Several books are filled with puppet performances aimed at the busy practicing librarian who doesn't want to spend too much time on puppetry. Therefore, this book does not cover making puppets to any great extent, but it does explain what to do with them once you've made them. Thanks to the late Nancy Renfro and a few others, there are also several excellent collections of in-the-classroom stories and performances that encourage children's participation and provide educational enrichment. Therefore, only a few scripts are provided in this book. In contrast, very few books provide details for making portable but professional stages. This book provides guidelines for two different types of stages.

Few books are intended for the public children's librarian or school media specialist interested in becoming a puppetry *performer* in the public library or media center setting. This book is intended for a librarian, library worker, or volunteer who wants to be better than mediocre or "just good enough to get by."

After having been a librarian for five years, I chose to become a puppeteer as well. I now have performed a few thousand shows over seventeen years. During this time I have shared stories and debated technique many times with my puppeteer colleagues. Although I have some fairly strong opinions about what works in puppetry for children and what doesn't, I always strive to give the reasons for these opinions. It is through thinking about what, why, and how we perform that our shows become fresher and better.

I'm going to try to convince you that puppetry is an excellent way to better communication with children, to help you find a role (even if only a limited one) as a performer, and to see puppetry as an oral art form. For puppetry is an art form—one that depends on your talent, on your voice, and on your audience and its reaction and, to a lesser extent, on the written work you've used as the basis for your performance.

Being a puppeteer requires a little something extra—a strong desire to reach children and the motivation to discover new ways to use that desire by developing performance skills. Most library staff who work with children have that desire but feel they lack the talent and training to begin performing. Others say, "I don't have time to make all those puppets." To those people I say: "Read on, and remember that in an oral art form, it's your personality, your style, and your desire to communicate that power the performance, not your props, puppets, or stage." Performers with the desire, a little confidence, good voice skills, and a good sense of timing can create a wonderful experience out of almost nothing (for example, out of puppets made of paper plates and Popsicle sticks).

An oral art form (like storytelling or puppetry) is not the same as a written art form (like poetry, stories, or editing others' work for print), but the two can work together wonderfully well. When you perform, you are both telling a story and creating it anew. You are also sharing the importance of language skills—of speaking and listening. The responses from the audience are a part of the performance—a part that empowers and motivates children who rarely get a chance to feel they have power. The children feel they have an important part to play in creating a work of words and actions. You are making literature real and relevant for them.

The best part of being a puppeteer is this direct effect you can have on the children in your audience. You can battle the shriveled imaginations that prerecorded entertainment on TV and videos gives kids. You can bring children, on a small but very effective scale, live theater. Watch their eyes, hands, and faces change when they see the Troll threaten the Billy Goats, or listen to the roar when they repeat the magic word that will turn a dog into a king.

The children remember a good performance, too. More than once a parent has told me that his or her child, who saw one of my shows at (for example) age three, still repeats lines from it at age five or sings songs from the show a year later. That's why it's worth all the building, adapting, and rehearsing. Read on, and try it for yourself!

1

Why Puppetry in the Library?

Producing and presenting an effective puppet show for children in a public library or school is a lot of hassle. It takes a lot of time, and there's a big risk something's going to go wrong and you'll feel like a fool. Yet schools and libraries are the places in which puppetry is healthiest today. Why? Let's imagine ourselves in a medium-sized suburban public library in Anywhere, U.S.A.:

In a closet next to the children's librarian's desk are a folded two-person puppet stage, a big bag of puppets and props, two sixty-watt clip-on lamps, a small portable public address amplifier, and two lapel microphones. The show is scheduled to begin at 2:30 this afternoon; it's now 10 A.M.

Marcia and Joanne, the children's librarian and children's-room clerk who have put together this modest version of "Little Red Riding Hood," haul the equipment out of the closet. They move furniture and set up the stage. They attach the Masonite and foam-rubber trees and flowers to the sides of the stage, pull the puppets out of the bag, and hang them from the hooks on either side of the inside of the stage, waiting for hands to slip inside them. The sound equipment and lights are clipped on, plugged in, and tested. Spare bulbs are at hand.

"Do we have everyone ready?" Marcia asks. "I've got Amos, Little Red, and Grandma, and you've got the Wolf and the Woodcutter."

Joanne asks, "Have you got Grandma's bed on your side?"

"Right here. Let's see if Grandma can set it up quickly and still look under the weather." (The puppets will be doing the scene changes in full view of the audience, so they need to remain in character.)

Marcia slips her hand into the Grandma puppet. She has Grandma pick up the foam-rubber-and-cloth bed from the prop shelf backstage, climb weakly up into view with her burden, set the bed onto the Velcro strip that attaches to the inside edge of the stage, and lie down on the bed.

Joanne, who has watched, says, "Maybe you should have her sigh a little after she puts the bed down."

"Good idea. How's this?" Marcia goes through the actions again, having Grandma reenter a little more slowly, ease the bed down, and give a tired little moan and straighten and slump before she gets into bed again.

"That's great."

"As long as you're there," Marcia says, "tell me how the flower scene works."

Grandma and the bed disappear. Ten seconds later, Little Red Riding Hood, her basket hung on her upstage arm, skips across the stage. Suddenly a honk is heard—Marcia is stepping on a small bicycle horn backstage—and a daisy shoots up into view.

Little Red stops and bends toward the flower, sniffs it, turns toward the audience, and says, "Ooh! Here's a nice flower! Grandma'll love it!" She bends from the waist, grasps it, and straightens up as she pulls the flower out and into her arms. Then she turns and skips off in the other direction.

The horn honks again, and another flower shoots up on the opposite end of the stage. Little Red says, "Another flower! I'll take this one too!" and pulls it up as well.

Two flowers in her arms, she turns again, and a third flower shoots up. "Another flower! I'll have a whole boo-kay for Grandma!"

Little Red bends and grasps this flower, but it refuses to budge. She pulls harder, walking backward, and the flower moves with her. She walks all the way back and forth along the stage, pulling, and the flower glides back and forth all the way with her, but it won't pull out.

Finally Little Red gives three great heaves, complete with small, polite grunts, and the flower pops out of the ground with such force that Little Red is thrown backward and vanishes, as if she's fallen inside the stage and is headed for the floor.

Marcia mentally counts "One thousand and one" and kicks a small box of metal bookends on the floor backstage; it sounds like a wastebasket full of ball bearings has fallen over.

All is silent for two beats; then Little Red slowly reappears, panting, but with the third flower in her arms. "I got it!" she wheezes. "Now *on* to Grandma's!" She skips offstage.

Joanne smiles. "That looked wonderful; those noises are great. The only thing to watch for is to make sure Little Red is really looking at the flowers when they first pop up. She says, 'There's a nice flower,' but she's looking at the side of the stage instead."

"Oops. I'll have to watch that. Why don't we run through the entire show now?"

The two puppeteers spend nearly ninety minutes rehearsing the show twice. These are the first rehearsals with all the props and scenery pieces finished. During the first run-through the puppeteers stop every few minutes.

A peg holding Grandma's house to the stage keeps coming loose and has to be fixed; the timing of Little Red's first meeting with the Wolf is worked out in detail, and the scene in which the Woodcutter opens the Wolf's belly (and in this version it's easy because there's a zipper) needs to be refined. During the second rehearsal they stop only twice to correct minor flubs. At 11:30 they quit, fold up the stage, move the furniture back, and go off to do what they jokingly call "some *real* work."

By 2:00 the furniture in the children's room has been shoved against the walls. Joanne and Marcia load the equipment on a book truck, wheel it out, and begin setting it up. As they work, the room slowly fills with children. By 2:30 there are at least one hundred children and parents.

The puppeteers clip on their microphones, turn on the amplifier, flip the stage lights on—there is a new sixty-watt bulb in each—and the library's storytime mascot, a bloodhound puppet named Amos, peeks over the stage.

Amos pops up and says, "Okay, all you guys. I know you're ready to see the story of Little Red Riding Hood, right?"

The audience says "Yeah!" in response.

"You know there's a scary Wolf in this story, right?"

"Yeah!" As they say it, the eyes of the Wolf pop up from the side of the stage. Several children shout, "It's the Wolf!"

Amos asks, "Where?"

The children point, "Over there!"

Amos looks, but there's no Wolf. "I don't see him."

The Wolf, by now, has popped up on the other side of the stage, looking as if he's about to take a big bite out of Amos.

"He's behind you!" The audience shouts.

Amos turns, but it's too late. The Wolf is gone. "He's not there. You guys are trying to scare me."

The Wolf is now behind Amos on the other side, and for the next half minute leads Amos on a merry chase, popping up all over.

Finally, the Wolf pops up at Amos's side, his mouth open, as Amos is saying to the audience, "You see? There's no Wolf here. Now, as I was—what are all of you yelling about?" Amos turns, looks directly at the Wolf, and turns back to the audience. "There's no Wolf, just like I—" Amos stops. "Oh-oh." He turns back, sees the Wolf, and yells "YAAH!" and runs off the stage.

The Wolf bows and says, "And now, ladies and gentlemen, the story of Little Red Riding Hood—and, of course, the Big, Bad Wolf. Heh heh heh." The Wolf slowly sinks out of sight, and the show begins.

Is Puppetry for You?

The preceding story is fiction, but puppet shows very much like this one are performed in libraries and schools all over the country every week. As the preceding example shows, a lot of effort goes into putting together even a simple program for children in a library or classroom setting. Puppets must be made or purchased, a script written or adapted and then rehearsed, voices and personalities for the characters developed, and scenes and movements worked out. The puppeteers need to practice until they feel comfortable with their characterizations, lines, props, and scene changes. If a prop breaks, it must be fixed; if a humorous bit falls flat, it must either be changed or thrown out.

Puppetry isn't for everyone, just as juggling or singing in public isn't for everyone. You must enjoy it, want to do it, and know why you're willing to devote so much of your time to struggling with scenery that won't let go of the stage when it's supposed to, sound effects that refuse to come in on cue, and puppets that catch on your clothes ten seconds before their entrance. Experienced puppeteers know why *they* do it: There is no better way to reach children.

Those who arrange and perform programs for children in a school or library know that there is something special about a puppet show. A well-done show—or even one performed passably but passionately—will light up every eye in the audience. After a few moments, the puppets will have almost any group of children shouting, laughing, booing (at the villain), singing, and even breathing together. Parents of three-year-olds have said that their children talked about the puppets—and little else—for days after a show. Few programs in public libraries draw children in such numbers and get them so involved; few keep them coming back in such numbers, bringing friends and neighbors with them.

Why does puppetry attract children so? Even in an age when they can see daily the most outlandish marvels on TV—singing robots, battles of alien spacecraft, people turned into monsters or vice versa—children feel a bond with a live performance that they can never receive from a video screen. There is always a feeling of distance watching a prerecorded program; there is always that glass window nobody can pass through. During a live show, no matter how simple, we enjoy feeling we are a part of it, that our participation—even if it's only our applause—makes a difference. There are no barriers between the audience and the performer except the performer's skill and receptivity to the audience.

There is something very satisfying in seeing children who normally spend hours every day sitting passively in front of a screen suddenly able to answer the puppets' questions, repeat magic words, or warn characters of danger. Added to this verbal bond is the visual magic of tigers, witches, or even chairs that talk to the children. These things are part of the reason puppetry attracts children, but there's still more to it.

What Is Puppetry?

What is puppetry? There have been as many definitions as there are books on the subject, but the simplest one is that puppetry uses objects as actors.

In the context of work in schools and libraries, however, it is probably better to define what puppetry is *not*. Puppetry is not building puppets, costuming puppets, making stages and scenery, or writing scripts. These activities bear the same relationship to puppetry as tuning a piano does to playing Beethoven or stringing a racket does to playing tennis. Puppetry is those special fifteen or thirty minutes you and your puppets spend making your audience laugh, gasp, and think. It is when all your preparation comes together into a performance and all the time and work you put into the show becomes worth it.

If you have ever watched the effect a good puppet show has on children, you shouldn't be surprised to learn that puppetry had its beginnings in religious ceremony. In fact, a little of the whiff of myth still clings to it. For centuries the Hindus and Indonesians have passed their religious traditions to a nonreading populace with puppets. Shamans of the Hopi and Kwakiutl people of North America used puppets in their ceremonies to amaze onlookers with miraculous transformations and manifestations of mythical powers and figures. For hundreds of years in European churches and cathedrals, puppets related stories from the Bible (a practice that continues in churches worldwide). Puppets function wonderfully as animate symbols in a way human actors cannot. They can personify abstract concepts and can simply and strongly communicate spiritual, magical, and other difficult-to-grasp ideas and feelings.

Communication through Puppets

Human actors have bodies, personalities, and emotions that are strictly their own and that color their performances; puppets can be made in any shape at all. Such transfigurations encourage puppeteers to discover a characterization for each puppet that is different from those of any others—like a body awaiting a soul. For example, a puppet snake skillfully handled can twist and curl and coil and show its forked tongue, and it will create a different, "snakier" effect than a human actor portraying a snake.

A puppet is a magical channel of communication, and puppetry, in its purest sense, is communication between the puppeteer and the audience through this channel. Using the magical channel of the puppet allows puppeteers to "disappear"—whether behind a stage or not—to lose their bodies and personalities and take on whatever form they choose, whether a mouse, a king, or a dragon. During a performance, the puppet has the eyes of all audience members; the puppeteer vanishes. How else can you explain the five-year-old who comes up after a show, sees you standing there with a puppet on your hand, and asks very seriously, "That was *you* doing the puppets, right?"

How can we use this channel of communication to its best advantage?

We need to understand how a young child experiences a puppet show. H. A. Rey's *Curious George* and its sequels have been popular with every generation of children for more than forty years because Curious George the monkey symbolizes the spirit of every young child learning his or her role in a world full of rules. Curious George wants very much to be good, but his natural urges to go places he shouldn't go and do things he shouldn't do always get the better of him. No matter how terrible his transgressions, though, the parent-figure of the Man with the Yellow Hat still loves Curious George and welcomes him back with open arms.

Children see the protagonists of most puppet shows that truly touch them much as they see Curious George. The puppet characters who appeal to them most—and look at Muppet characters like Kermit the Frog and the Sesame Street characters of Big Bird, Bert, and Ernie as examples—are those who are learning how the world works. The characters want to do the right thing and be successful and loved, but they make mistakes along the way just as the children (and all of us, really) do. These characters are challenged by villains, by inanimate objects that seem to have minds of their own, or by problems that take every drop of their ingenuity to solve. They flounder but triumph in the end. They are abstractions and simplifications of their audience, and in creating any puppet presentation you should consider how the protagonist's struggles and successes mirror those in the life of each child watching the show.

The children in your audience follow the puppet character as it tries to find a place in the world. In such a show children learn and listen eagerly, becoming emotionally involved with the story unfolding on the small stage. In many puppet plays, even the smallest and mildest characters can defeat giants, perform mighty physical feats, and control outcomes with magic words and powers. Children watch these feats hungrily, wielding the powers vicariously.

This free identification with the spirit of the puppet can lead to some disturbing violence at times. Children sometimes become so emotionally involved in the show that they rush the stage trying to grab and strike the villain while yelling insults. Often, when I come out after the show with a puppet or two to meet the children, some of the children seem compelled to punch or pull on the puppets, almost ripping them. This tendency to behave violently with puppets seems to occur most frequently, however, when a child puts a puppet on without a clear idea of what to do with it. Even the mildest-looking bunny or duckling can become a devouring monster or kung-fu expert on the hand of a six-year-old. The puppet here is once again like Curious George—it can get away with anything, regardless of the consequences. The puppet is like a small id at the end of the child's arm, and it gives a feeling of power and freedom to a child who works hard (most of the time) to restrain strong impulses to yell, punch, kick, and generally act up.

Marie Noe of the Abilene, Texas, Public Library sees the same thing happening, even when she is the one wearing the puppet in a storytime or after a library performance. "For some reason the first thing children—and some adults—do when presented a puppet is to jam their hands into the puppet's mouth and yell, 'Bite it!' That is something I actively discourage."

This same emotional "freedom" children experience with puppets allows them to open up with puppets as they never could with adults. The puppetry literature is full of cases of physically or sexually abused children describing how they had been abused and how they feel to a puppet or with the puppet's help. Other children who are too emotionally disturbed to speak with unfamiliar adults have slowly begun talking with a puppet operated by a caring teacher or social worker. Children with terminal illnesses have found it easier to discuss their worries and feelings with a puppet worked by a hospital therapist. Puppetry can be powerful stuff; it's not just fooling around with bunnies and frogs.

Four Kinds of Puppets

As previously mentioned, making puppets is not puppetry. Yet you must have puppets of some kind or there is no show—and the kind of show you will be able to perform, the stage you will need to use, and the capabilities of your characters will be largely determined by your puppets. The four major kinds of puppets are hand, string, rod, and shadow puppets. All four can be as simple or complex as you wish to make them. This book is mainly concerned with hand puppets and, to a lesser extent, with rod puppets, but the basic principles presented should be useful with any kind of puppet. Some people are naturally drawn to one type of puppet over another due to personal taste or talent, but all have their special virtues and disadvantages.

Hand Puppets

Hand puppets have always had a special appeal to young children because there is no barrier between the puppeteer's body and the body of the puppet. Once you stick your hand inside, every movement of your fingers, thumb, wrist, and arm automatically and directly becomes a movement of your puppet's hands, neck, waist, and body.

There are two basic kinds of hand puppet: the *glove puppet*, in which one of your fingers and your thumb become the puppet's arms and another finger supports the head, and the *mouth puppet*, in which your fingers and thumb work the puppet's mouth. Mouth puppets have become popular largely since the advent of television, because they look more natural when seen close up, as on a video screen; the Muppets are of course the best-known examples. Hand puppets have little cousins, *finger puppets*. These are puppets that fit on individual fingers. They are lots of fun in individual play and in intimate groups such as preschool storytimes, but their size makes them useless in most performance situations.

Hand puppets are at their best when worked broadly and almost instinctively. They are excellent for slapstick, for handling props, and for portraying fables, humorous folktales, and other stories that are simple, brief, and to the point. They are probably the best puppets for interacting directly with the audience, partly because the visceral pleasure of direct control of the puppet makes improvisation easier. Children want to put the hand puppets on and work them too.

The biggest disadvantage of hand puppets, however, is the human hand that gives them life. Hand puppets, if cleverly built, can vary a good deal in size, but they can't be too small for a hand to fit inside or too large for a hand to hold them up and control them. If an elephant and a mouse are hand puppets, they will need to be approximately the same size. A hand puppet princess will always need to be a little stout or else wear a voluminous gown if a fist is to fit inside. In addition, without a great deal of engineering talent, the hand puppet's form does not allow legs and feet that can be worked. Thus actions involving walking, running, flying, and dancing can only be suggested, not shown directly. Unless very skillfully made and manipulated, hand puppets are also perceived as comic characters by most people; therefore, they are difficult to use dramatically.

String Puppets

String puppets, or marionettes, are the "class act" of puppetry. Their con-struction—a hinged body and limbs hung from and controlled by as few as two to as many as twenty fine strings—encourages fine, delicate manipula-tion that requires a good deal of practice. String puppets tend to be more artistically sculptured, taller, slimmer, and closer to the human form than the squatter, more lumpish hand puppets; therefore, string puppets are more often used for performances aimed at adults. Most puppet productions of Shakespeare have used string puppets. Until about 1950 most professional and many amateur puppeteers worked primarily or exclusively with string puppets; a far smaller proportion uses them today.

Children find string puppets fascinating. However, because string pup-pets are operated from a distance using a hand-held control that does not correspond with the shape of the puppet itself, and because they are hung from strings that tangle easily if they are operated with any real enthusiasm, children often find all but the simplest string puppets frustrating to use. With practice and determination, however, children from about fourth grade up can learn to master string puppets and get them walking, jumping, and flying through the air while hand puppets remain earthbound.

Rod Puppets

Rod puppets might be considered a cross between hand and string puppets. While they can be tall, dignified, and delicate like string puppets, they are controlled from below and anchored to performing on the stage. Rod puppets can be quite large and have outlandish shapes, and they lend themselves well to portrayals of folktales, comedy, drama, and almost any other kind of literature. Stick puppets are the simplest variety of rod puppets and are no more than two- or three-dimensional figures mounted on single sticks. Rod puppets usually have two or three control rods and require both of the puppeteer's hands to operate, which is a disadvantage if the puppeteer is working alone or if many characters are needed on stage simultaneously. Like string puppets, rod puppets require a great deal of practice to be manipulated believably.

However, there are many uses for rod puppets in libraries and schools, particularly those of the stick-puppet variety. For small animals, such as insects and mice, stick puppets are necessary so a hand puppet elephant or lion can be in proper scale. Furthermore, for storytelling with puppets, in which characters need to be rapidly picked up and put down, stick puppets are also very useful.

Shadow Puppets

Shadow puppets are perhaps the oldest as well as the most mysterious kind of puppet. They are related to rod puppets but are used very differently because the puppets themselves are never seen. Figures cut from paper, leather, plastic, or other materials are hinged, attached to rods, and manipulated behind a brightly lit translucent screen. With added bits of colored plastic gels for accents, shadow figures can be startlingly beautiful. They are best used with older children and adults to portray myths, legends, and other material with a feeling of "long ago and far away." In skilled hands, though, shadow puppets can lend a wild new dimension to comedy.

With some practice and experimentation, one or two shadow puppeteers can erect and destroy cities in a matter of seconds; a whole crowd can be manipulated by one person, and the figures themselves can easily break into pieces, float upside down, and grow huge and tiny as they are moved closer to and farther from the screen. Not every puppeteer can be successful at shadow puppetry—it requires a special kind of discipline and taste—but every puppeteer should at least try it.

Puppetry as Art

Whatever type of puppet you use, keep in mind that puppetry is not frivolous, even at its silliest. It's an art form in the same class as opera, ballet, and mime. Because puppetry can also be an effective educational tool that is very attractive to children, many people who want to be sure that children *really* pay attention to their message come to see puppetry only as a convenient means to an end, not as an end in itself. Many puppet shows presented in schools these days have ulterior motives as subtle as whoopee cushions: The presenters' goal is to teach children about fire safety, disabilities, or not to talk to strangers. In the effort to get the message across the presenters often pay little attention to the quality of the puppetry itself. While shows in libraries are rarely this didactic, some shows exist only to push a particular book or to promote reading in general, and it appears that such puppeteers have forgotten how to tell a story simply and joyously.

Children can learn easily and absorb much from puppets, but they do it best when the message is only a portion of a package that includes humor, strong characterizations, a good story, and a real desire on the part of the puppeteers to communicate and entertain. "Entertainment" is still a dirty word in some educational quarters, as if children cannot learn something important from a well-done performance without an obvious educational goal. Too much concentration on educational goals robs puppetry of its true reasons for existence—achieving a bond between puppeteer and audience and communicating ideas and feelings that the puppeteer truly wants to share. Without this desire to share and communicate, puppetry can never be an art; it will be only a dry and passionless craft, no matter how beautifully the puppets and scenery have been built and how cleverly the special effects are performed. With the desire, one puppeteer with a paperbag puppet can keep audience members on the edges of their seats and in stitches.

2

Developing Technique

Many staff people in schools and libraries sometimes think about being puppeteers, but they feel self-conscious about standing in front of a group of children, talking in a funny voice, and fooling around with a puppet. Few people can grab a puppet and charm the socks off their first audience. Occasionally they will, but often nerves and lack of practice are all too evident.

Beginner's nerves are nothing to be too concerned about. Your ultimate success as a puppeteer will have little to do with how much of an extrovert you are and how much experience you have as a performer when you begin. Natural self-confidence never hurts, but if it is lacking, it can be developed. In fact some of the finest and funniest professional puppeteers are painfully shy without a puppet in their hands. Library staff who choose to work with children, over those who work with adults or those who work in nonpublic departments such as technical services, tend to have at least a little ham in them. Slice that ham; serve it up to the children. Preparation and discipline are important, too.

The Performer's Attitude

The real key to doing well as a puppeteer comes in your perception of yourself as a performer. Puppeteers who want to succeed should always hold a few fundamentals in mind:

They have something worthwhile to share.

Performers must have faith in their own talent and desire to perform. They don't have to believe they will be the greatest puppeteers in history, or even the best in town. However, they are strongly motivated to share ideas, to tell stories, and to make their audiences laugh and cry and think.

They always will try to improve, to refine, and to grow.

Once performers are satisfied with the quality of their work and stop working at being just a little better next time, their ability to truly reach their audience begins to fade. They must constantly be looking for new ideas, new stories, new performance media, and new ways to turn a witch into a cat and back again.

A puppeteer's most important goal is to build a bond with the audience.

Every puppeteer needs to listen to the audience while performing. Which stories, jokes, routines, and characters are working, and which aren't? Which shows are working with which age groups and cultural groups? Which performances surprise an audience, move them, let them feel they are party to a little secret between the puppets and themselves? Always listen to the audience's reactions and watch (whenever possible) the audience's eyes and body language. The audience is constantly giving feedback about the performance.

They view each performance as an opportunity to communicate with their audience.

Without a message or a goal, a performance is meaningless. The message doesn't need to be anything earthshaking. By sitting in front of a preschool storytime group with a frog puppet, asking questions about the weather outside, and commenting on the clothes children are wearing as they are welcomed, the librarian/puppeteer is telling the children, "Hello! I'm glad you're here!" and helping them feel comfortable in a group. Successful puppeteers always know *why* they are performing and *what* the performance is telling the audience.

Developing a performer's attitude helps you tell yourself and others that you're serious about what you're doing, even if you're only a beginner. Thinking seriously about these fundamentals as you progress in your work will help you measure your development as a performer. However, this does not mean that you need to dedicate your life to puppetry. You are a librarian or teacher first, a puppeteer second (or third, or whatever, depending on your other talents and interests). As long as you take your performing seriously, even when you're trying to make your audience laugh, it will put talking in funny voices and fooling around with a puppet in front of a group into a whole new dimension.

Creating Your Characters

The best puppet performances are those in which the audience gets to know a small group of sharply drawn, clearly differentiated, complete characters and to watch them interact. The characters' voices, the way they move, the language they use, the way they react in different situations, and the way they look are all equally important in identifying one character as the hero or heroine, another as the villain, and still another as the hero's friend or the villain's comic assistant. If you think of each puppet as the outward reflection of a complete character, you can begin the work that makes each successful puppet characterization "real" and not just a funny voice reciting lines from a script while a puppet is moved more or less simultaneously.

Whenever you first pick up a puppet that plays a particular role in a show, ask yourself some questions about that character:

How old is the character?

Is the character intelligent, dim, or somewhere in-between?

How does the character treat friends?

What was the character doing just before its first entrance?

Dream up as many questions such as these as you can, and answer them as definitely as you can. Write the answers if you need to.

For example, if you are using a story like "The Three Billy Goats Gruff" as the basis of your show, you may think you know the answers already, but ask the questions anyway. Even very familiar stories don't tell you everything you need to know about the characters. You know that the Troll is mean, growly, and grumpy, but—and here is how you create *your* Troll—is he that way because he feels like the world hates him and he needs to act tough in return? Is he simply a big, cocky bully who thinks that *nobody* can beat him? Is he a dopey, devouring monster who is long on appetite but short on brains? The story communicates that the Big Billy Goat is strong and determined, but we know next to nothing about the other goats except their relative sizes and the pitch of their voices. Is the Little Billy Goat childlike? Crafty beyond his years? Is the Middle Billy Goat cowardly? A slick wise guy? Many well-known folktales use their characters more as plot devices than as real personalities, so it's up to you to interpret and flesh them out.

After you have considered your character's personality, you are ready to put your puppet on your hand and ask yourself two more questions. Given the character's size, shape, and role in the story, how does it speak? How does it move? Let's concentrate on the voice first.

Breath Control and Voice

To gain greatest control of your characters' voices, you must first learn to control your own. If you project your voice and articulate your words, the little girl on the far right-hand side of the last row will be able to understand every word you say. To project your voice, you must speak as if the breath that supports each word began in the pit of your stomach. You need to use the muscles of your diaphragm, concentrating on and grasping each sound with your lungs and larynx, supporting it with each breath the way a singer does. Many people without public speaking or performance training speak only from the upper portion of their lungs; without proper breath support their voices are thinner, shallower, and less flexible than the voices of those who speak from the diaphragm.

Relaxation is also very important; speech should never sound tense or forced. Too much tension in the chest and throat cuts down on volume and flexibility as well.

If you lie on the floor and hook your hands under your lowest ribs while counting "One, two, three" aloud in the fullest, richest, most relaxed voice you can muster, you will feel your diaphragm at work. Take some deep breaths and stick out your stomach as you inhale; then breathe as you usually do. How much difference is there between the two voices? Breathe again with your stomach, easing out any words or sounds that come to mind—"La, lo, lee, loo" or "I wish I were a wooden watermelon" will do as well as anything—as clearly and distinctly as you are able. If you can, go into an auditorium or other large room with a tongue-twister verse like Laura Richards's "Eletelephony," and read it aloud with full breath support. Look at the last row or the far wall. As you read, do you feel every word reaching that point without strain?

Phrasing

If you will be speaking lines for more than one character in the same scene of a show, you must also consider your ability to phrase, to break sentences and conversations into easily manageable segments. A clarinetist playing a long passage of music often notes the places to take breaths so that each musical phrase gets full breath support. You won't need to make "breath marks" on your scripts, but as you learn dialogue, emphasize different combinations of words and syllables and think about the best way to phrase each line. Following is a scene of dialogue intended to be performed by one person working both puppets, showing one way it might be phrased to stress the differences between the characters and the rhythm of the scene as a whole. Strongly accented words are in bold type, and breaths are marked with a plus (+).

Moe and Joe are at the door of a haunted house. Each wants the other to go in first.

MOE:	OK, here we **are**. + I'll follow **you**. +
JOE:	No, **you** go first. *(gets behind Moe)*
MOE:	**No**, after **you**. + *(gets behind Joe)*
JOE:	No . . . + after **you**. *(gets behind Moe)*
MOE:	**No**, after **you**. + *(gets behind Joe)*
JOE:	I in**sist**. *(gets behind Moe)*
MOE:	No, **I** insist. *(gets behind Joe)*
JOE:	**No**, I in**sist**. + *(gets behind Moe)*
MOE:	**Hey**, look over **there**! *(points out at audience)*
JOE:	+ Where? + *(looks)*
MOE:	**Here**! *(gets behind Joe and shoves him through the door)*

The dialogue itself is minimal, yet the action can be very funny if broken into rhythmic phrases, subtly communicating that Moe is a little pushy while Joe is a little on the dim side. The tempo should gradually accelerate from the first line to "Hey, look over there!" and pause just a beat at "Where?" with the climactic shove following immediately.

Voices for Multiple Characters

If you are working both characters, you must carefully rehearse a scene like this. Not only must you speak the lines distinctly in two easily distinguishable voices but you must establish a rhythmic pattern of both voices and actions and carry them to a quick climax. Breath support for both characters must be strong, and breaths must come at the right times.

Many beginning puppeteers feel uneasy about creating "funny voices" for their characters and maintaining them throughout a show. Exploring your voice's potential becomes easier, however, when you understand its dimensions. Every voice has a dimension of pitch (from high to low), volume (from loud to soft), rhythm (from fast to slow with all sorts of accents and syncopations between), and a more amorphous "fourth dimension" of quality, which includes everything from a raspy, nasal croak to a rich, orotund Shakespearean actor's voice.

It may help to picture these four dimensions in a diagram of possible voices, with your own natural voice at its center. (See figure 2.1.) The diagram is made of the three intersecting axes of pitch, volume, and rhythm, surrounded by a circle of qualities. In the center is your natural voice; surrounding it are the three directions in which you can "stretch" it (volume, pitch, and rhythm), which are overlaid with qualities you can add (gruffness, clarity, whininess, etc.).

Each "funny voice" you create will have its place in the diagram. For example, a voice for a big, grouchy bear will probably have a low pitch,

■ FIGURE 2.1 Dimensions of the Human Voice

slow rhythm, and loud volume, and have a gruff quality. A timid mouse's voice would be the opposite in pitch and rhythm and have a squeaky or whispery quality. To gain maximum control over your voice, test your full range in each of the four dimensions (pitch, rhythm, volume, and quality). Try changing your voice from loud to soft, from high to low, from fast to slow, and speak with every quality you can imagine. Stretch your voice to its limits; then find the limits of comfort.

Once you have explored your entire range, you will be ready to give a puppet its voice. The voice should come to you almost intuitively after thinking about the character the puppet is to portray, its personality, and its size and shape. If the character's voice doesn't come to you, relax, close your eyes, and imagine yourself as that character, doing what it must do in the story and looking the way it does, and then speak for it. The voice you discover may not be far from your natural voice. However, chances are you will discover a voice at least slightly higher or lower, louder or softer, faster or slower, or different in quality from your own. Following are some tips for developing voices for your puppets.

A character's voice should be comfortable for you.
You might, with a great deal of effort, be able to squeeze out a sepulchral, roaring voice for the Troll, but if you find yourself fighting off the urge to

cough and clear your throat after five minutes of dialogue, don't use that voice. Moderate one or more of its dimensions until you feel you could speak in that voice for an hour if necessary.

A character's voice should be distinct from all others you use in a show.
Differentiate voices by using opposite ends of the dimensional scales for different characters. You might, for example, give one of the Three Little Pigs a high, gruff voice; another a fast, whiny voice; and the third a slow, soft voice. The Wolf might have a low, clear (but craftily syncopated) voice. Don't differ the voices just for the sake of differing them, though; your Three Little Pigs should each have a different personality to go with each voice. If the voices don't feel right for the characters, you will easily confuse the characters' voices as you change from one character to another. A voice is not separate from the rest of a character. It is one part of a complete "puppet personality," and it should not be interchangeable from one puppet to another. For example, I have several puppets that I use in a number of shows, but each has the same voice and basic personality regardless of the show. This consistent welding of puppet, voice, and personality makes it very difficult to lose or confuse voices, even during fast-moving dialogue.

One character's voice should be as clear and well-articulated as all others in a show.
Stay away from accents and dialects unless you are *extremely skilled* at performing them. Even then, such features aren't really necessary in most shows. The same effect can be created by varying the rhythm of a character's speech and the lines.

Always keep your audience in mind when you present a character with a particular voice.
Accents and dialects may offend audience members from that region or culture. Also, *never* use speech irregularities such as lisps or stuttering as part of a character. Using such voices makes fun of those irregularities and also makes a character harder to understand. In addition, if you are performing in places like public libraries or child-care centers, be aware of children with disabilities involving hearing or language or those who aren't native English speakers.

Manipulation—A Puppet's Body Language

Voice is only one facet of a puppet character. Another facet, equally or, in some stories, more important, is movement. Each puppet character should be made to walk, react physically to events, and physically express an emotional state in an individual way. How convincingly each puppet character acts and reacts depends on how convincingly you manipulate it. Following are important characteristics of a well-manipulated puppet.

The manipulation will make the audience truly believe the puppet is alive.

The audience should not think that the puppet is a toy that someone behind the stage is moving with his or her hands. It should appear to be maintaining eye contact with whomever is speaking—the audience or another puppet. It should stand up straight and remain at a constant level in relation to the stage, not sinking or leaning as the puppeteer gets distracted or gets tired of holding it up. If it is a mouth puppet, its mouth should move only when talking, and it should always move its mouth when it *is* talking.

The puppet will tell a story through movement and what it says.

If the story calls for a puppet to be tired, the puppet should move lethargically, dragging itself along the stage, leaning against the scenery, and heaving its body as it yawns. If it's a sneaky character and is skulking around, it might peek around the scenery for a moment, only to duck and hide when another character looks in its direction, or bob up and down jerkily as it runs across the stage, as if tiptoeing.

All puppet movements in a show should be rehearsed well in advance; to develop your manipulation skills, try to think of at least two ways your puppet can perform the same action. How many ways can the Three Billy Goats trip-trap across a bridge? How many ways might the Wolf sneak up to meet Little Red Riding Hood? The ideal amount of movement will have the puppets moving smartly and clearly every time they need to, not so little that they look frozen or so much that they are constantly jiggling around and distracting the audience from the story.

The puppet will stay in character even if it isn't the speaker or the center of attention at the moment.

If another character is speaking, the first puppet will be watching that other character, perhaps nodding or shaking its head subtly in reaction to what is being said. If another character is dancing, digging a hole, or trying to swat a fly, the first puppet will be watching that character and clapping in time, moving its head along with the shovel, or jumping a little each time the swatter strikes the stage.

Hand and rod puppets must behave as if there is a floor beneath their feet all the time.

As you rehearse a show, decide on a "floor level" for your characters—the height at which you will hold them. (See figure 5.4 in chapter 5 for an idea of where to establish the floor level.) As your puppets go through their paces, monitor their heights constantly. It sounds difficult when you have so much else to do backstage, but with practice and experience it becomes second nature. It is especially critical that you watch the levels of your puppets when several are onstage; you don't want your lion looking up at your mouse.

Eye Contact

As briefly mentioned earlier, eye contact gives your puppets the illusion of life. A skilled puppeteer is always aware of where and at whom the puppets are looking. Your audience will be looking where the puppets are looking, so carefully plan the direction of your puppets and the turning of their heads as you rehearse. For example, suppose two puppeteers have three puppets onstage simultaneously. If one puppet character is speaking, the other two puppets should be looking in that character's direction. (See figure 2.2.) The eyes and faces of the two puppets who aren't speaking draw our attention to the one who is. Notice that in figure 2.3 you can't tell which puppet is the speaker and the center of attention because no character is the focus of the action.

■ **FIGURE 2.2**   Correct Eye Contact with Speaker

■ **FIGURE 2.3**   Incorrect Eye Contact

It's easy to get distracted backstage if you have a prop that falls off the prop shelf or a piece of scenery that looks as if it's about to come loose. At such times it's hard to pay attention to where your puppets are looking and what they're doing. However, it's these distracting lapses that break the illusion of life on your stage, so train yourself to keep the correct eye contact among your puppets even if you're trying to pick up a wayward prop with your foot.

Mouth puppets present manipulation problems of their own. Once again, be aware of where your puppet is looking. Most mouth puppets if held in a relaxed position (particularly if you perform while sitting) will be looking into space, and the audience will only see their lower jaws. Become aware of your hand. As shown in the trained position in figure 2.4, you'll want to bend your hand down accordingly.

Hand Positioning for Glove Puppets

When performing with glove puppets, be as aware of your puppet's hands as you are of its eyes. Because of the shape of the human hand, your glove puppet, if held in a completely comfortable position, will look like the victim of a robbery with its hands in the air. Train yourself to fight nature by holding the thumb and finger that slip into the puppet's arms down and in as shown with the second puppet in figure 2.5.

Unless your hands are built *really* funny, there is no way to hold a glove puppet's arms down to its sides; instead, a good position consists of holding the arms straight out in front or resting against the character's chest. This position should be the "rest position" for your glove puppet while onstage, during whatever time it isn't involved in strenuous action or dialogue. Every other action it makes—picking up a rock, dusting the furniture, shooing away a cat, or waving its arms as it recites a magic spell—should be crisp and definite. Watch in a mirror as you make your glove puppet go through

■ **FIGURE 2.4** Mouth Puppet Hand Position in Natural and Trained Positions

"NATURAL" HAND POSITION FOR MOUTH PUPPET (INCORRECT)

"TRAINED" POSITION (BETTER)

"NATURAL" HAND POSITION (INCORRECT)

"TRAINED" POSITION (BETTER)

these actions, or have someone videotape your puppet performing them. If you weren't manipulating the puppet yourself, would you be able to tell what it was doing?

Figure 2.6 shows how the major joints in your hand correspond to the anatomy of a glove puppet. With the puppet on your hand, think about which joints must move to perform a particular action. A puppet picking up a prop shouldn't lower its whole body until its arms hit the stage. It should bend from the waist (your wrist) smartly, grasp the prop in its arms, and straighten up while your wrist and arm remain at the same height relative to the stage. This consistency creates the illusion that your character is standing on a real floor as it bends down. A puppet who is running or jumping will use its "legs and feet"; in other words, you use your entire arm, including your elbow and shoulder, to make the movement. Waving and nodding are

■ **FIGURE 2.6**   Anatomy of a Glove Puppet

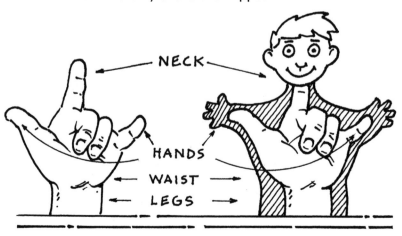

NECK

HANDS

WAIST

LEGS

finger movements, but if your character shakes its head to say "No," the movement will need to come from the wrist and the puppet will rotate its entire body.

Mouth Puppet Manipulation and Voice

Learning to coordinate the words you speak with the movements of your puppet's mouth isn't easy, but some practice can bring a lifelike illusion of speech. When human beings speak, our lower jaws move. On a mouth puppet it seems natural to move your fingers, but since they control the upper jaw, moving your fingers will give your speaking puppet an unnatural "head-flapping" motion. You can compensate by pushing your hand very slightly forward on the syllables you wish to emphasize, as shown in figure 2.7. Don't exaggerate this motion, but if you're subtle about it, it will liven up the speech of your mouth puppets.

The hardest part of natural-looking speech with a mouth puppet is knowing how much emphasis and mouth motion to give each line of dialogue. Too much concentration on mouth motion can make your puppet look awfully busy. If you make a mouth puppet say "antidisestablishmentarianism" and try to make the puppet's mouth open and close on every syllable, you'll wind up with a cramp in your hand. Human mouths tend to open more during vowel sounds and close on consonants, but that method won't work quite so well with mouth puppets unless you have your puppet saying a lot of things like "Ohhh!" and "Shhh!" As you say your lines, it works a little better to open and close the puppet's mouth on the accented syllables ("<u>once</u> up<u>on</u> a <u>time</u>").

While speaking the words with your own mouth, imagine you are simultaneously shaping the words with your hand. Vary how widely you open the puppet's mouth by the emotional content or volume of the speech. For most normal conversations, your fingers and thumb should never be

■ **FIGURE 2.7** Mouth Puppet Speech Movement

MOUTH CLOSED, HAND BACK

MOUTH OPEN, HAND FORWARD

more than two inches apart. Diligently practice speaking with a mouth puppet while watching in a mirror, with the puppet turned to face you, or by reviewing a videotape of the practice session. Making acceptable speech movements with a mouth puppet is not an easy skill to master, but it is a very important one.

You should also practice using the head of your mouth puppet to perform many activities besides speech, much as you would the head and body of a glove puppet. Since most mouth puppets don't have functional hands, they must pick up and manipulate props with their mouths, using their neck joints (your wrist joints) as a glove puppet would use its waist. On long-necked or long-bodied mouth puppets like dragons, snakes, and geese, practice using all of your arm to slither, rear, or waddle. The more skillfully you use your fingers, wrists, and arms, and the more you feel your joints working together in an organic whole, the more lifelike your mouth puppets will be.

Entrances and Exits

How your puppets will enter and exit your stage will depend on two things: the way your stage is built and the mood of your show. I perform with a small Punch-and-Judy-style booth with an open proscenium and no wings. (See figure 5.4 in chapter 5.) If your stage has wings, your puppets may enter like human actors, at full height from the wings. But if your stage has no wings, your puppets must either mime climbing stairs up to the visible stage area or simply pop up. The "climbing stairs" method is certainly the only one to consider if you are performing a dramatic story or a dignified folktale. With a light fable, a comic fairy tale, or a slapstick skit, "popping up" adds to the humor of your show.

Some critics say that having puppets pop up out of the floor is a mark of a poor puppeteer, but I disagree. A centuries-old street theater tradition has puppets entering and exiting by popping up and down. Furthermore, by varying the manner in which puppets pop up, you can establish the characters from the beginning. For example, a shy character might rise slowly and tentatively, peeking over the stage first; a more aggressive character might roar out of nowhere, or a jaunty frog or hare might bounce up to the stage and vibrate as it hits the visible stage area to stop and speak.

Experiment with entrances and exits to find a method that works best for you. Refine it and use it consistently. Remember that whether your characters climb into view or pop up, once they've arrived (as paradoxical as it sounds) the imaginary floor level remains there—"solidly" in place—until they leave.

3

Script Writing
and Adaptation

If you are new to puppetry, you'll have a lot of basic skills to learn in a short time—character creation, vocal flexibility, manipulation, and simple showmanship. Most beginning puppeteers who are also librarians or teachers will not want to add writing an original show to this list. Instead, they will adapt at least their first few shows from well-known picture books or folktales. They are wise to do so. Adaptations of well-known stories are almost always easier to perform for several reasons:

Since your audience already knows the story, they will find your performance easier to follow. They will thus be more comfortable and ready to participate. Don't underestimate this benefit in an age of TV-induced short attention spans. You'll be able to concentrate on creating whimsical versions of well-known characters, working little twists into the famous plot, and encouraging the audience to take part in the performance.

By being more comfortable with a well-known story, your performing will feel more secure. A story you've known since childhood or have read to children for years will be a story you can step into easily when you put your puppets on. Even if you've written an original script, you still must learn it, create completely new characters with new personalities for it, and find the rhythms and climaxes of your language and plot. This all takes time.

A well-known story, particularly a folktale or fable, has been tested over time. It has proven psychological and emotional validity for young audiences. Not only will you be positively affecting your audience with a well-performed version but you'll also be building your self-confidence as a performer when the children let you know how much they're enjoying it. In contrast, with an original script, the audience will need to work harder at following the story and getting to know the characters, and they'll have less time to react. If the emotional "logic" of the story isn't just right, their reaction may be confused or half-hearted.

Elements of a Good Script

In all my years in puppetry, I've written only five completely original shows—usually to fit the special themes of summer reading programs. The creation and rehearsal of each of these shows took roughly twice as long as adapting a familiar story. After completing what I thought was a "final" script, I've discovered that whole sections of dialogue had to be added or discarded once rehearsals began. Sometimes a plot that looked wonderful on paper failed to get much reaction from the audience at the first performance and required a major overhaul before the second. Therefore, if you write an original script, prepare to work harder and risk a less-than-overwhelming response. Whether you write or adapt, the same parameters apply to any show: physical considerations, audience considerations, and language and plot.

Physical Considerations

How many puppeteers will be performing, how experienced are they, and how much time will they have to prepare? The typical school or library puppet show performed by adults or adolescents uses two, or at the most three, puppeteers. You will thus have a maximum of four or six puppets onstage at once; this means you will have difficulty performing "Snow White and the Seven Dwarfs" without a very cleverly written script. Even with four or six puppets to work with simultaneously, remember that your blocking (the movement of characters around the stage) gets exponentially more complex with every added puppet. Most classroom and library stages are small, and even if you *can* have six characters onstage at once, they may not be able to do much more than stand in a line and talk. (See chapters 4 and 6 for other considerations when staging a solo show and performing in a library.)

Audience Considerations

With younger audiences, keep the script simple. The ideal show for ages three through eight

- has five or fewer total characters
- is thirty minutes long or less
- has no more than three scene changes
- has very simple props and scenery

A classic example is "The Three Billy Goats Gruff." It has only four characters (no more than two of whom are onstage at any one time), only one necessary piece of scenery (the bridge), and no scene changes. The original story is very short and very accessible to even the youngest children, but it can be expanded and customized easily without losing its fundamental "rightness." "The Three Little Pigs," once you add the two extra pieces of scenery to make three houses, is also relatively simple to produce. Both stories need only basic dialogue to communicate the plot and have lots of action potential. Stories such as Nonny Hogrogian's *One Fine Day* (Collier, 1971) or *The Teeny-Tiny Woman*, on the other hand, work better in the format of storytelling with puppets (see chapter 4) because the beauty of these stories depends more on their language than the action. The puppets in these latter two stories serve more as a visual focus for the flow of words than as actors, and the stories don't lend themselves to customizing.

Language and Plot

Remember the three Rs of literature for young children—rhythm, rhyme, and repetition. All three help a young child learn a story, understand how a plot progresses, and feel the music of the spoken word. Everyone who works with young children knows how fingerplays and repetitive songs work their magic. They know that many popular stories go through the major plot actions three (or more) times. In "Goldilocks and the Three Bears" there are three bowls, chairs, and beds. "The Three Billy Goats Gruff" includes three dramatic crossings of the bridge, and "The Three Little Pigs" includes three encounters with the Wolf. Young children need and enjoy this kind of repetition and the rhythm it holds; it gives them the security of knowing how the story works and gives the plot time to assemble itself in their minds. This understanding of simple plots lays the foundation for the comprehension of the more complex stories they will soon be encountering in school and in pleasure reading.

Use repetition liberally in your scripts. When I began performing "The Three Billy Goats Gruff," I followed the story, in which the Big Billy Goat knocked the Troll off the bridge once, and that was that. The audience, primarily preschoolers, didn't react much, as if everything had happened too fast for them. As an experiment, I repeated the bout twice more with slight variations at the next performance, and the children loved it. By the third time the Troll got pounded, the children were whooping and cheering. The Big Billy Goat and Troll have gone three rounds ever since.

The plot of a puppet show for young children should be like a can of evaporated milk—pure and concentrated. Avoid subplots, unnecessary characters, or long descriptive speeches. Never have characters tell something if they can *show* it. The plot should develop clearly from the beginning (in which the main characters and their situation are introduced) to the middle (in which the characters are challenged or challenge each other) to the end (in which the climax is reached and the problem resolved). Having a sleek plot doesn't mean you can't have the characters sing songs or go through some slapstick routines, but make sure each song or routine develops the story or enriches the characterizations.

Original or Adaptation?

Literary purists—those who feel that preserving the story in written form is the highest priority—and academics will no doubt feel that you have no right to make many changes in a story. However, puppetry, like storytelling in its original form, is an oral rather than a written art form. I would never make changes in a story created by an author—when I tell Don Freeman's *Beady Bear* (Viking, 1954) or Nonny Hogrogian's *One Fine Day* (Collier, 1971) with puppets, for example, I am extremely faithful to the originals.

On the other hand, no folktale exists in only one form. Folklorists have collected untold numbers of variations of the same story. In each one, the storyteller stresses some things, leaves out others, adds little twists, and improvises from the audience's reaction. Modern storytellers will take a story and make it their own, and the audience will judge how well they have molded and interpreted it. The strengths and limitations of puppetry will also influence the amount of story adaptation to some degree, for without talents and engineering abilities beyond the average amateur, puppets cannot do everything people can or everything presented on the written page. Yet much of puppetry's charm lies in such limitations.

Most of my script writing has been to adapt "generic" folktales—shows in which it doesn't matter if an author's specific language is used in the script. To adapt one of these tales, read several versions to find your "own" version of a story, using the basic story line and sprinkling it with ideas of your own. With the plethora of children's—and adult—folklore collections available these days, this is the route to take when adapting folktales.

Adaptation and Copyright

At times you really may want to adapt a specific version of a tale, for example, Jon Scieszka's *The True Story of the Three Little Pigs* (Viking Kestrel, 1989) or one of the Reys' Curious George books, to make it into a puppet show. One question surfaces over and over when the question of adapting copyrighted material is discussed: Do you have to get permission from the author or publisher? For many years, when I converted one of Arnold Lobel's Frog and Toad stories into a brief puppet show as part of a Valentine's Day Friends program, I felt, "Well, as long as I'm not performing the show for profit, who cares?" Now I no longer do it. No doubt many of us sincerely believe that a use of a story that promotes that story—and may even sell more copies of the book as more children hear and enjoy it—isn't going to bother the author or publisher, right? Imagine a buzzer going off and an announcer saying, "That's incorrect!"

The current U.S. copyright law awards a copyright holder—such as the author or illustrator of a children's book—the exclusive rights of reproduction, adaptation, publication, performance, and display of that person's creative work. Two of those rights—those of adaptation and performance—particularly concern us here.

For a more complete description of the complexity of complying with the copyright laws, read Janis H. Bruwelheide's *The Copyright Primer for Librarians and Educators* (American Library Association, 1995). However, just to give you an idea, the right of adaptation means the "right to prepare a derivative work," including a dramatization, whether you publish it for profit or not. If you adapt H. A. Rey's *Curious George Takes a Job* (Houghton, 1947) or a chapter from Arnold Lobel's *Frog and Toad Are Friends* (Harper, 1978) into a puppet script, you are breaking the law unless you have received permission from the copyright holder.

The right of performance is the "right to publicly recite, render, play, dance, or act it." *Publicly* means "in a place open to the public or a place in which 'a substantial number of persons outside of a normal circle of family and its social acquaintances are gathered.'" In other words, adapting and performing Jon Scieszka's *The True Story of the Three Little Pigs* (Viking Kestrel, 1989) in a typical library or school situation without getting permission from the publisher or author is breaking the law twice.

The majority of children's services library staff in this country are breaking the law all the time. (I say this not to chastise anyone, but to admit reality.) We love the books we promote; we want to share them with the young people we serve. However, copying illustrations from a picture book and making them into flannel board figures for your toddler storytime or being videotaped by the local cable channel while reading a copyrighted book or poem without getting permission is breaking the copyright law.

The guiding principle in using copyrighted material seems to be, "Is my use of this copyrighted material depriving the copyright holder of profit?" In most cases, the answer is no when performing in a school or library in which admission is not charged. This is one of the factors considered in fair-use guidelines, covered in Section 107 of Title 17 of the U.S. Code. The chances of anyone "coming after you" if you use copyrighted material without permission are very remote, but it's illegal to do so all the same.

Unless you can make a strong argument that your use of the material qualifies as "fair use," you are required by law to obtain permission.

Requesting Permission

How do you obtain this permission? Usually you get it through writing to the rights and permissions department of the book's publisher and asking for permission, stating exactly how you plan to use the work.

Getting permission takes time. When I wrote for permission to read a group of picture books aloud on a videotape for our local cable channel, it took five weeks to get a response from the publishers. Several publishers wrote back—in some cases months later—saying that they no longer held the rights or that I would have to write to the British publisher to get the rights. Several publishers never responded at all. Most library staff who have written publishers for permission report better luck than I had, though, and most publishers granted permission with no problems and at no charge. However, some ask a fee of $25 or $50, so be prepared.

You can usually request permission via e-mail these days; check with the publisher's Web site to see if there is an e-mail address for the permissions department. However, even using e-mail doesn't guarantee a rapid reply.

Perhaps you are saying to yourself at this point, "Phooey. I'm not going to bother getting permission for every puppet show I do. I'll stick to folktales that are in the public domain." Ah, but *are* they in the public domain? In libraries we're surrounded by folktale books, but every one of them is copyrighted in the name of the reteller. If you use Paul Galdone's *Little Red Hen* (Seabury, 1973) as the source of your puppet version of that story, are you breaking copyright law? Definitely, if your script uses Galdone's exact words or your scenery looks like his illustrations. As mentioned previously, read several versions of any folktale you're interested in adapting, and you'll soon learn which words are part of the traditional telling and which are the reteller's.

If you're in any doubt about any of the preceding, don't rely on anything written here—check with an attorney. Copyright and "fair use" of copyrighted materials is a hotly contested area.

Adapting a Story

If you work in or near a library, you are surrounded by stories ripe for adaptation. For the beginner in puppetry, two excellent places to begin are Anne Rockwell's anthologies of basic nursery stories, *The Three Bears & Fifteen Other Stories* (Crowell, 1975) and *The Old Woman and Her Pig & Ten Other Stories* (Crowell, 1979). These are collections of elementary stories everybody should know, and they adapt themselves easily to puppetry. With a few of the basic stories adapted, performed, and under your belt, you will be ready to move farther afield into Russian, African, Chinese, and Native American stories. These are more work because the feeling of another culture affects the plot and performance style; however, they can be extremely satisfying once mastered.

When you are browsing through the hundreds of anthologies of folk-tales available and come upon a story that *might* be worth considering, immediately write down the tale's title and the anthology's title along with any thoughts about how you might use it. When you have narrowed your possibilities down to two or three, read each story twice and ask yourself:

> How many characters are there? How many of the characters are absolutely necessary to carry the story? If there are a large number, might any of them be eliminated or combined? How many characters are onstage at a time throughout the story?

> How much of the story hinges on dialogue and language alone, and how much on action? How does the dialogue sound when read aloud? Will it be necessary for any characters to deliver long speeches or descriptions or to tell long stories for the plot to make sense? How difficult is the vocabulary?

> What are the possibilities for humor and conflict? Are there actions in the story that can be "drawn out" into funny or exciting bits of business? Are the hero's and villain's motivations clear, and can they be translated into the voice and movements of your puppets so that any child in the audience will know almost immediately who is the hero and who is the villain?

> How many scene changes and props will be absolutely necessary to tell the story? How many might be eliminated or combined without harm to the plot? Will your puppets be able to handle the necessary props and perform all the necessary actions? (If you are using hand puppets, and the plot calls for your hero to rise into the air on a flying carpet, you had better be prepared for some long nights in your workshop.)

> Will the story make sense to the intended audience? Is the situation one with which they can identify? Will they need any background information (about Chinese culture, for example) to understand and enjoy the story?

After you've evaluated a story and it still looks attractive, list the characters and how they look and act in the story, the necessary pieces of scenery and scene changes, the necessary props in each scene, and a brief telegraphic synopsis of the plot. These are the puppets, scenery, and props you will need to make, find, or buy and the story you will tell with all these things. Appendix A includes five tales I've adapted using these methods. Following is an example of the preliminary planning I went through after deciding to adapt the story "The Three Little Pigs" to a puppet show. (The revised/completed version appears in appendix A.)

ADAPTING "THE THREE LITTLE PIGS"

Adapting a particular story that many children know well is, in its way, as tough as adapting a story that none of them know. Children bring to the show plenty of their own expectations about how the story is going to play itself out, and if the puppeteer is going to deviate from that story, he or she needs to demonstrate that this different version is worthwhile, too. For example, when I decided to do a one-person production of "The Three Little Pigs," I began with the standard plot but saw problems with it.

> *Plot Synopsis* Introduction—First Little Pig enters, sets scene, looks for way to get house
>
> *Scene 1* First Little Pig meets Man, gets straw, builds straw house; Wolf comes, blows house down, chases First Little Pig
>
> *Scene 2* Second Little Pig enters, looks for house, meets Man, gets sticks, builds stick house; Wolf comes, blows house down, chases Second Little Pig
>
> *Scene 3* Third Little Pig enters with bricks, builds house, settles in; Wolf comes, tries and fails to blow house down
>
> *Scene 4* (inside brick house) Wolf says he's coming in; Third Little Pig puts pot in fireplace; Wolf falls in after trying to come down chimney and gets cooked for supper
>
> *Conclusion* good punch line?

I was planning to construct glove puppet pigs so they could handle props, but having the pigs actually build the three houses was going to be difficult. I thought about starting each scene with the house built and the pig ready to move in, but I wanted to show how each pig, with his own personality, went about obtaining his house. So I opted for a magical solution: the first two pigs would use a magic word to create a house with no work. Like most magical creations, these houses wouldn't be built to last. How would the pigs get the magic word? This would be the role of my master-of-ceremonies puppet, Artie, who would introduce the show by practicing his magic tricks (and not doing very well). The Third Little Pig, of course, would spurn the magic word in favor of practicality—he would order a prefabricated brick house, *guaranteed wolfproof*, with the money he had saved.

So far so good, I thought. But what about the climax, in which the Wolf gets boiled in the pot? Because of a complaint about violence in a show I had recently performed, I felt it might be better to take care of the Wolf another way. Having already introduced magic into the plot, why not have the Third Little Pig, with great reluctance, use the magic word to transform the Wolf into something small and harmless? It seemed worth a try.

In addition, it would have been very difficult to bring the Wolf down the chimney and into the pot without building an interior scene and forcing another scene change on the performance. Neither would boiling the Wolf have been in the silly, nonsensical spirit of this version of the story. Who is to say which Wolf suffered more in the end—the Wolf boiled in the Pig's pot or the proud, sarcastic Wolf who found himself transformed into a tiny mouse and became prey instead of predator? Even a slapstick story works better for children if its "emotional logic" holds it together.

I wrote a draft script, which I used to develop the final script. It varies quite a bit from the original folktale, but I believe it still follows the spirit of the tale. (See appendix A.)

Reading the script for "The Three Little Pigs," you will probably notice that the characters spend a lot of time saying hello and goodbye to one another, repeating the magic words, and talking about the actions they are about to perform. In actual performance these lines are "tossed off" with little emphasis, but they are there because the play is usually performed before preschoolers—some as young as two—and young elementary-school children. These lines assure the audience that the story is easy to follow, and the names and relationships of the characters are repeated often enough that the children know who everyone is, that the actions (like the ritual of using the magic words) are learned well enough that the children can begin joining in early in the show, and that the children are never lost. Remember that your show just might be a young child's first experience with live theater, and it should be comfortable and easy to follow.

Sensitivity Issues and Classic Tales

As seen in the previous example of dealing with the Wolf in "The Three Little Pigs," adapting classic fairy tales is often problematic. At times it seems that no matter what you do, you're going to offend somebody:

"The Three Pigs" is too violent for small children. The Big Bad Wolf gave my son nightmares.

"Little Red Riding Hood" is too sexist because she has to be saved by a big, strong man. You should show women as the heroes.

The little girl in "The Gunniwolf" disobeyed her mother. I'm trying to bring up children who honor their parents. Do you know how hard that is today?

We're not staying to watch "Hansel and Gretel" because there's a witch in it. It's against our religious beliefs to expose our children to witchcraft.

Complaints like these aren't common in your day-to-day life as a librarian or performer, but they will come your way every once in a while. Many parents, child-care staff, and teachers are very concerned about what ideas and images the children under their care see and hear. Many adults see the school and library as refuges from the TV violence, amorality, consumerism, and the endless spawn of tacky "licensed characters" children see on every channel and in every store. Puppetry can offer a wonderful alternative to the homogenized mindlessness of mass entertainment, but to truly engage a young audience, a performance must include conflict, tension, and emotional release.

Violence

Violence has a fundamental place in puppetry for young children, but it needs to be handled carefully. Many folktales are violent; some are so violent in their original versions that the ones we find in the children's collections today have been well expurgated. Cinderella's stepsisters in the original version wanted to fit into that glass slipper so badly that the first stepsister cut off her own toes, and the second her own heel; both were discovered by the blood in the slipper. The Wicked Queen in the original version of "Snow White" was sentenced by Snow White and the Prince to dance in red-hot shoes until she fell down dead. Many children do not know that in most versions of "The Three Little Pigs" the Wolf eats the foolish first two pigs (the Disney version seems to have won the day).

We use folktales today with children much younger than those for whom they were intended; their original audience was a community of adults and children of all ages whose lives regularly included violence and death. Even so, read Bruno Bettelheim's *The Uses of Enchantment* (Random House, 1976) or talk to any group of five-year-olds and you will realize that violence is never far from the dreams and imaginations of most children.

Today's hand puppetry traces its ancestry to the British Punch-and-Judy show and its European relations—shows so violent and sexist that they are practically unperformable today. In the "classic" Punch-and-Judy show of the years 1800 to 1850, Punch throws his crying baby out the window; beats his wife Judy to death; murders a policeman, a neighbor, and a stereotypical black servant; fools the hangman into hanging himself; and kills the Devil after a mighty battle. It was not a show designed for children, although children watched it being performed in the streets along with everyone else. As the nineteenth century ended and the twentieth began, Victorian influences mellowed the violence, and the show became a mildly naughty children's entertainment that is still seen throughout Britain today. A few American puppeteers perform shows with the Punch and Judy characters, but their scripts are very different from the classic show.

Nevertheless, Punch has survived so long because he has been something people enjoyed—a character sort of like an R-rated Curious George. Punch does things many people secretly wish they could do—not murdering people, perhaps, but doing whatever things he wants whenever he wants to do them—and he gets away with them. He does terrible things (in a funny and inimitable way), and the audience still loves him.

Did the violence of the classic show affect the audience—particularly the children in the audience—adversely? Probably not; in fact, many historians of puppetry believe the murder and mayhem of the show were therapeutic. If this doesn't sound convincing to you, recall that the street puppet show, like the basic library or classroom show, is performed in an environment that stresses its abstraction and unreality as well as the feeling of "it's only a show." Characters who are "murdered" will get back up and run through their paces at the next show. The performance leaves the audience with a silly but satisfying catharsis, not the tension one receives from watching the kind of violence in a film or TV show that aims for a close reconstruction of reality.

This does not imply that any librarian/puppeteer can or should perform the original script of "Punch and Judy" for a preschool audience, or even that your puppets can clobber each other once in a while without you hearing about it from the parents. However, when puppeteers try to totally eliminate violence from their shows and make political correctness their first priority, some spark of life is almost always lost. There is something inspiring about watching a character struggle and beat a challenge, and something satisfying about seeing a villain humiliated.

On the other hand, violence, even comic violence, may not be for you, and I do not tell you that you should use it. However, I defend its occasional use in adaptations of folktales that include violent acts—not the blood-and-guts style of horrific violence, but the violence of Fox eating Henny Penny and Cocky Locky offstage or the Troll and Big Billy Goat Gruff battling their eternal battle.

It's not difficult to imply all sorts of violence without having a single violent act onstage. Often the simple threat is quite sufficient. Your Wolf can snarl, show his teeth, and growl, "Then I'll blow your house *down!*" and he'll have the children holding their breaths. Rumpelstiltskin can suggest the direst horrors as he dances around in the forest, cackling that "the Queen's baby will be mine, *mine, MINE!*"

In some stories violence, or the threat of violence, is needed to further the plot. It needs to be clear, however, that the violence brings misfortune to the perpetrator of the violence or that it comes about from wrongdoing. In my adaptation of the Sioux story "Coyote and the Galloping Rock" (see appendix A), Coyote, who believes that "rules are for other people, not for me," commits an injustice against the cultural rule "what is given is given" by giving his blanket to the Rock and then taking it back. The Rock later asks for the blanket back and warns Coyote that he will regret it if he doesn't return the blanket. When Coyote refuses, the Rock pounds Coyote flat—into a talking "coyote-skin rug." It's very clear to the audience that Coyote gets what he deserves.

If you have your characters actually do battle, it's not difficult to choreograph a fight that is comical enough for any audience to digest. The Troll and the Big Billy Goat face each other. The Big Billy Goat is serious and determined; the Troll is ragging him mercilessly: "Nyaah, nyaah. Come on and hit me!" The Big Billy Goat charges, the Troll leaps out of the way, and the Billy Goat hits the other side of the stage and falls. The Goat shakes himself, gets up, and charges again. The Troll leaps out of the way, laughing again, as the Goat hits the side of the stage and falls again. As the Goat picks himself up, the Troll leans out to the audience and chortles, "That old goat couldn't hit the side of a barn. What a bean-brain!" The Troll is so puffed up with pride that he fails to notice the Goat charging once more, and the Troll is knocked into orbit. Watching a fight is the most fun (and the least disturbing) if it has a little plot—a sequence of events all its own.

Most of us love experiencing violence vicariously and safely through the arts; it satisfies something deep in our genes, even while we claim to dislike it. Young children are no different from the rest of us; in fact, they glory in mayhem. It's up to adults—as bizarre as it may seem at first thought—to give mayhem reason and form without lessening its impact. In our work as storytellers and puppeteers, we can give children the kind of conflict they need most to see—conflict in which right triumphs over wrong, in which the small hero succeeds through hard work and talent over the big, nasty villain. Especially today, children need to watch the good, the hard-working, and the willing-to-learn characters win out. In the classic fairy tale, such characters always do.

Villains

Don't make the villains too mild. They need to appear mean and rotten enough to present a real threat to the heroes. The best puppet villains for young children are melodramatic hams; they leer, growl, and cackle. They bully and threaten the childlike heroes and take great joy in doing it. The villains can talk down to the heroes, laugh at them, and act as though the heroes could never find the wit or ability to thwart them. When the heroes defeat them, the villains are shocked, which makes their defeat even more fun.

The only thing your villains should *not* do is leap out of nowhere, roaring and baring their teeth; this will frighten many younger preschoolers to the point of tears. In contrast, children love it when the Wolf sneaks up behind the hero, ducking out of sight when the hero turns around. The children will warn the hero, but the hero will never see the villain until the last moment. The audience loves being able to see a threat the hero cannot. This game of peek-a-boo needs to be tightly choreographed, however; if the hero turns and sees the villain ducking, the illusion is shattered. To achieve this surprise, it's best if one person works both characters. If two puppeteers are working, they should rehearse by tapping beats or counting so that both know exactly when to turn, rise, and fall.

In any puppet script that works and has a villain, the villain needs to be soundly defeated and humiliated. Make the villain look foolish at the climax, for that's what every proud, blustering bad character deserves. When he gets knocked off the bridge by the Big Billy Goat, the Troll howls to the accompaniment of a loud crash backstage; when he returns, dizzy and shaken, the Big Billy Goat picks him up by his nose and flicks him back off effortlessly. In my adaptation of "The Three Little Pigs" (in appendix A), the Wolf, so proud of his teeth and his cleverness, is changed into a mouse by the Third Little Pig and runs away in terror. Don't bother trying to reform the villains of classic folktales; it almost never works. The children *want* to see the villain get his just deserts.

Gender

The issue of fairy tales and gender roles is another kettle of fish whose aroma comes to mind if we and the parents we deal with are at all sympathetic to feminism. It is unfortunately true that most of the best-known folktales reflect the traditional sex-role stereotypes—the striving, heroic prince who saves the passive, suffering princess, and so on. However, stereotyping is not all-pervasive in folklore; the past twenty years have seen the publication of several excellent collections of folktales featuring active women. Also, there are a few that have always been on our shelves: "The Little Red Hen" works hard supporting her lazy friends until she asserts her independence; "Molly Whuppie" slays a nasty giant; and the "Three Strong Women" from Japan is excellent for both storytelling and puppetry.

As for the other stories—the ones we want to perform, even if we don't like their politics—we are free to make a few subtle changes that shift the heroine's characterization, but we should always be careful not to mar the story's basic message. For example, "The Gunniwolf," which is based on an Indian tale, has a traditionally passive heroine who narrowly escapes from her encounter with fierce animal energy. When I adapted it for a puppet show, I made the Little Girl a strong, mouthy sort who blithely ignored her mother's warnings and didn't discover until too late (when the Gunniwolf appeared) that she was in big trouble. The Little Girl didn't let that stop her; after discovering that she could lull the Gunniwolf to sleep by singing, she taught the audience her song. Then she convinced them—leading them lustily, swinging her arms to keep time—to keep singing long enough for her to make her getaway. The stronger heroine did not alter the story's message, but she made the story a lot more fun to perform.

To stress the point again: as a performer, you are allowed to interpret. So long as you find the essence, the spirit, of a particular story and work out how you are going to share that spirit with your audience, the details of the story need not be unchangeable. If you are unsure of the changes, be cautious and try them out with a test audience—any of the children you know and work with regularly will probably be happy to share their feelings with you—before the first "real" performance. You need to share a story you believe in and can present confidently.

4

The One-Person Puppet Program

Very few puppeteers begin by giving one-person shows. It's much easier, especially when you're starting out, to have at least one other person to share the construction of puppets, props, and scenery; the writing of the script; and the tossing around of ideas. By working with another person you have someone to be nervous with before the show and someone to share the responsibility for the performance.

Unfortunately, it's difficult for many (if not most) librarians, media specialists, and teachers to find a colleague willing to work with them and spend the kind of time necessary to put on a good show. Librarians who work with young people have very little free time to begin with. People's work schedules clash, and they want to have some time for a real life that doesn't involve work. The result is frequently a program that, despite the best intentions, is underrehearsed and feels dissatisfying. If you find yourself in this position, and don't mind taking on a creative challenge, solo puppetry offers some very real advantages (as well as some very real limitations).

You have complete creative control.
All decisions regarding the style of the show, setting, characterizations, voices of the puppets, script, and colors of the scenery and costumes are yours to make. On the other hand, it also means you have complete responsibility for everything, including the task of selecting or writing a story that one person can perform effectively and then actually performing it. A solo performance can be difficult if your characters must handle many props, there are a number of scene changes, or more than three or four

puppets are required and you will be putting them on and taking them off throughout the show.

You are free to improvise during a performance.

If the urge strikes and the audience is receptive, your characters can deviate from the script and make jokes or talk about people, places, books, or TV shows the audience knows. Improvisation will stimulate your creative abilities and sharpen your wit. It'll make you a better performer who will be ready for anything as long as you are also prepared for the possibility you'll fall on your face.

You are far more flexible about scheduling performances.

With nobody else's schedule to cause conflicts, a small portable stage you can carry yourself (see chapter 5), and a few puppets you can throw in your car (or even just a tote bag of puppets and props for storytelling), you can carry your show anywhere. You can perform in other libraries or classrooms, at community festivals, and even at children's birthday parties. Skilled solo puppeteers who are willing to tour their communities can become an important public relations person and cultural ambassador for the libraries or schools.

The Puppet Mascot

The best way to begin as a solo puppeteer, particularly in a school or library, is to create a puppet mascot and use it regularly whether or not you plan to perform full-scale shows. A puppet mascot should be a character who reflects both a little of your own personality and the world view of a child in your audience. If you work primarily with three- to eight-year-olds, you should use a puppet character that is easy for young children to identify with. Mascot characters should be cute, but not *too* cute; they shouldn't be threatening, too bland, too large, too small, too perfect, or too grotesque. Frogs, homely dogs, and "cute" monsters all work well as mascots. Your mascot should, once again, be like Curious George—basically decent, with a sense of right and wrong and a desire to do the right thing, but with some difficulty in suppressing those urges to be the center of attention and praise. It will show off, brag, and do and say things without thinking sometimes but will also learn from mistakes and try to do better next time.

Puppet mascots can be used with or without a stage, but they are at their best on your lap as one corner of a triangle of you, the puppet, and the children. Because they are often used away from a stage, they should be complete figures, including legs, feet, tails, or whatever. They might also be in a "container" that can sit on your lap (a nest for a bird, a small spaceship for an alien or robot, or—in that hoariest of clichés that is nonetheless new to each group of young children—a book for a bookworm) and into which you slip your arm. Mouth puppets seem to work a little better than glove puppets as mascots, probably because conversing with you and the children is their main task.

Many teachers and librarians, however, use silent or "whispering" mascots: the rabbit or mouse who is "too shy to say anything," so it whispers everything into the puppeteer's ear, and the puppeteer repeats it to the audience. Such puppeteers may use silent mascots because they feel they must be ventriloquists to speak for a puppet without a stage. This is *not true*. You do not need to be a ventriloquist—just energetic, with a well-developed puppet personality at the end of your arm. If you believe in what you're doing, and you treat the puppet as a living being—look at it when it speaks, and react to what it says—the children will watch the puppet's lips when it speaks, not yours. Limiting yourself to a whispering puppet mascot will constrain what you can say and do and diminish the amount of fun you can have with your audience.

One of the best ways to use a puppet mascot is as your "assistant" during classroom or library storytimes. With your puppet on your hand, greet the children by name and talk with them about the weather or their clothes or about whatever holiday is near. You and the puppet will speak to each other, and you will both speak to the children. Your goal, whatever you talk about, will be to welcome the children, make them comfortable, and set the mood of the program.

Puppet mascots can also be useful in other parts of your job. As a children's librarian in a public library, I have used mine to visit schools and talk to classes about the library and its services, to introduce special programs given by colleagues or hired performers, and even once as a speaker in a news conference that kicked off a library funding election. If you use your mascot often and well, children will come up to him before and after programs to hug and kiss him and ask him interesting questions. They will also come up to you in the grocery store and ask you where he is. You may also discover, as I have, that your mascot can become sort of an alter ego, reflecting aspects of your personality that never otherwise reach the surface in your everyday life.

Sample Introductory Dialogue

For several years I used a bright green bullfrog puppet named Henry to introduce my public library preschool storytimes. Each week we had a little conversation before the first story. Here is a sample dialogue from a Halloween story program that was followed by a mask-making session.

LIBRARIAN: Good morning and welcome to storytime.

HENRY: (*on librarian's lap*) Hi there! Pull up some floor and make yourself homely. You know what day it is tomorrow, don't you? It's Christmas!

CHILDREN: No. It's Halloween!

HENRY: You can't fool me. It's the Fourth of July!

CHILDREN: No. Halloween!

HENRY: You're wrong. It's Mother's Day.

CHILDREN: No! Halloween!

HENRY: Aw, nuts. I can't fool you guys. You're too smart for me.

LIBRARIAN: Henry, did you get a costume to wear?

HENRY: Yes! I've got the scariest mask in the world.

LIBRARIAN: Really?

HENRY: Yes. It's so scary I don't even like to look at it. Do you want to see it?

LIBRARIAN: I don't know. Maybe not, if it's **that** scary.

(to children) Do you want to see it?

(Henry starts nodding enthusiastically)

CHILDREN: Yes! Yes!

LIBRARIAN: *(to children)* Don't you think you'll get too scared?

CHILDREN: No!

LIBRARIAN: All right, then. Let's see the mask, Henry.

HENRY: Oh, boy! Just a second. *(jumps off librarian's lap into a paper bag by the side of the chair,*

grabs the mask there in his mouth,

hops quickly into Librarian's lap with his back to the children so they can't see the mask,

and tries to talk)

Mmmumbhumpfummn.

LIBRARIAN: What? Oh, you want me to help you put it on?

(Henry nods)

All right. *(puts it over Henry's face)* There you are.

HENRY: *(still turned around, with mask on)* OK—here we go. One . . . two . . . three . . . **Boo!** *(turns around wearing a cutesy-poo bunny mask)* Are you scared?

CHILDREN: No!

HENRY: Oh. How about this? *(jumps up and down, making "scary" noises)* **BUGGA-BUGGA-BOO-BOO! RRROWWWHOO!!** *(finally quits, shakes off the mask, and sits there, out of breath)*

LIBRARIAN:	You'd better forget it, Henry. You're not going to scare anyone with that mask.
HENRY:	But the man in the store said it was the scariest mask in the world.
LIBRARIAN:	I think he was fooling you. Why don't you make your own scary mask? We'll be making masks right after the stories are over.
HENRY:	That sounds like fun. But right now, I'm going to sit in my bag and listen to the stories. Bye, everybody!
LIBRARIAN:	See you later, Henry. *(puts him in bag)* Now let's start with our first story.

The dialogue and action are simple, yet they get the children involved and thinking about the subject of the storytime. Other special occasions, like the first day of spring, National Hat Day, Grandparents' Day, or any other celebrations you can pull from *Chase's Calendar*, can lend themselves to similar dialogues. Once every year, during September, a holidayless month (well, Labor Day isn't a holiday children get excited about), we celebrated Henry's birthday. He wore a pointy party hat and passed out treats to the children.

Whatever the occasion, my puppet mascot always introduces the program and then is put away until the end to say goodbye until next week. He "sits and listens" in his bag when I need my hands free to hold books and manipulate flannel board pieces.

Improvising

When creating an introductory dialogue with a puppet mascot, think of it less as a written script and more as a framework for a three-way improvisation. Use only a few props (if any at all), and have everything within easy reach. If the children are to participate in the dialogue, stick to yes-or-no questions until you know them very well and they are totally relaxed with you. When working with preschoolers and kindergartners, you will get lots of non sequiturs if you begin by asking questions that require more of an answer than yes or no. (For example, Puppet: What animal has a long trunk, big ears, and lives at the zoo? Child: My mommy took me and my sister to the zoo yesterday.) Don't be afraid to follow the conversation wherever it goes—you will learn some amazing things about the children in a free-floating discussion—but you must be able to take control of the conversation and lead it back to the original subject.

Sometimes, though, improvised conversations will help you develop your puppet character in an almost stream-of-consciousness fashion. Once, in a storytime introduction about the places people live, the children started talking about their houses. The conversation started getting rowdy with three children talking at once, and to regain control Henry chimed right in with an improvised description of his house in the swamp. I hadn't given it any thought before that second, but out it came anyway—Henry's kitchen table was a giant mushroom, a turtle delivered his mail (that's why it took him so long to get letters), and there was always a foot of water in the living room. There was a noisy alligator family living next door; one played a piano that was full of water, and the other sang like a garbage disposal.

Storytelling with Puppets and Props

Another simple but effective use of solo puppetry is storytelling using puppets and objects. Many "mainstream" storytellers—the sort who teach in universities and write articles in professional journals—discourage storytelling with objects or visual aids like puppets or flannel boards. They call for oral telling only, believing that a child's imagination should not have to lean on crutches. Unfortunately, many of the children a librarian or teacher works with today have been so heavily subjected to "visual aids" like TV and videocassettes from an early age that many of these children have difficulty absorbing a story without some kind of visual focus. Storytelling with puppets and props might be considered a mutant child of puppetry and storytelling. Puppets and props can help the child of the video age make the transition to purely oral storytelling.

I prefer to see such storytelling, however, as a hybrid performance art of its own that operates with its own rules. It demands more performing ability than that needed by the purely oral storyteller and demands more involvement with pure language by the puppeteer. Both presenters may see it as a chance to "stretch" their talents. It is also a performance art ideally suited for the teacher or librarian who is used to being the whole show herself, who has too many responsibilities and too little time. Puppets and props you can hold in your hands as you tell a story give you a focus; if you're nervous, they give you something to do with your hands, and they remind you of the events and characters in a story.

Applications for Storytelling

Some stories work very well with puppets and props, and others do not. Short, humorous stories, such as fables and "noodlehead" stories, are ideal. Stories with fewer than five characters, like Aesop's "The Hare and the Tortoise," or stories like Nonny Hogrogian's *One Fine Day* (Collier, 1971), in which one character meets a succession of other characters, work better than epic tales with seven dwarfs or twelve dancing princesses. Humorous ghost stories, like "The Big Toe" or "The Teeny-Tiny Woman," work better than really scary ones.

Every Halloween I like to tell the story of "The Green Ribbon" in which a girl always wears a green ribbon around her neck and a boy has to know why, so he sneaks up behind her, unties the ribbon, and her head falls off. I have a simple glove puppet of the girl with a removable head made from a Styrofoam ball to which the green ribbon is attached. As I tell the story, I play the part of the boy as well as the narrator. For the climactic scene, I hold the girl puppet in one spot, facing the audience; as I speak, I sneak slowly around behind her, grasp the ribbon and pull it off—and the head comes with it. The audience usually gives a little gasp until I stand there as the boy, shoulders bent, the girl puppet's head dangling from the ribbon in my hand, and end the story with an "Oh-oh." This gets a good laugh and breaks the tension. It's simple stuff, but it's a great way to grab the attention of a class full of fourth-graders at the beginning of a program.

Puppets for Storytelling

Since most puppets used in storytelling, as opposed to a show with a full stage, are only "on" for a minute or so, it doesn't make much sense to create fully three-dimensional figures. Instead, try using stick puppets, figures cut from two pieces of tagboard, then glued and stapled over a foot-long piece of quarter-inch dowel, as shown in figure 4.1.

If you make stick puppets of human or animal faces about nine inches high, they also will double as masks, allowing you to change your identity easily as you tell a story. If you wanted to tell *One Fine Day*, for example, you might use a mouth puppet or glove puppet for the fox with a tail held on by Velcro and use stick puppet masks for all the other characters except the grass of the field and the water of the stream, which should be played by the children in the audience with you prompting them.

■ **FIGURE 4.1** Stick Puppet Example

GLUE BOARDS
TOGETHER, DOWEL
IN MIDDLE — STAPLE
ON BOTH SIDES OF
DOWEL FOR STRENGTH

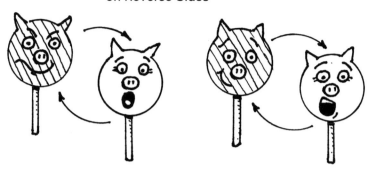

■ **FIGURE 4.2** Stick Puppets with Different Facial Expressions on Reverse Sides

You can use the two sides of each stick puppet, putting different facial expressions on each side, and turn the puppet around at a critical moment in the story. You might want to do a version of "The Three Little Pigs," for example, in which the faces of the first two pigs are smiling and smug until the Wolf blows their houses down, after which they are quickly turned to show expressions of exaggerated terror, as shown in figure 4.2. The Wolf might look nasty and have a frown until he blows their houses down, after which he revolves to show an evil smile of delight.

Three Bears with Two Hands

With stories involving more characters than you are able to hold in your hands at one time, you can recruit children from the audience as helpers. Stories with repetition, stories with "add-on" characters like "The Turnip," and very familiar stories like "The Three Bears" or "Little Red Riding Hood" are best for this kind of telling, especially when you're just starting out. For example, as you tell the story of "Henny Penny," pull out the puppets of Henny Penny, Cocky Locky, and the others and bring volunteers up to hold them and go through the actions. You play the part of Foxy Loxy and use two chairs back to back and about a foot apart to represent Foxy Loxy's den. Lead the children inside to "eat" them (taking back each of their puppets while making a loud chomping and smacking noise, then sending them back to their seats).

If you plan to enlist the help of preschoolers, be sure they know you well enough to feel comfortable standing in front of the group. Once a cheery visiting librarian/storyteller asked for a volunteer to play a chicken and no preschoolers would come up. She saved the day by getting all the children to be chickens, then roosters, and so forth. Flexibility is always a virtue in working with young children.

Trick puppets add occasional spice to programs. Try a telling of Cynthia Jameson's version of "The Clay Pot Boy" (Coward McCann, 1973) using paper head, feet, and arms taped to a partially inflated balloon to represent the Clay Pot Boy and small stick puppets for each of the characters he eats. As each person or animal is consumed, pass them behind the Clay Pot Boy and give the balloon, which you have been pinching shut, a good lungful of air. By the time he meets the Billy Goat, the Clay Pot Boy should be enormous. The Billy Goat should have a needle taped near his horns, and charge enthusiastically into the balloon. I guarantee you a grand climax and audience members on the edges of their seats. After the balloon pops, hold the remnants of the puppet in one hand as one by one you lift up the characters and things the Clay Pot Boy had eaten with the other hand and show them to the audience. End the story slowly and quietly to bring the children back down to earth.

Another example of having three puppets onstage at one time in a one-person show is shown in the photo. In this scene from "Issun Boshi" or "The Inch Boy," a Japanese folktale, a fisherman rescues Issun Boshi after he has fallen into the river. The Issun Boshi figure is made of a piece of wood that has been dressed in a costume, and the fisherman needs to pull him out of the river before a hungry fish gobbles up the boy.

Staging Your Solo Show

Working as a solo act requires all the performing skills you can muster. You'll need always to track where your eyes, your hands, your feet, your puppets, and your props are and to be aware of what the audience is doing as well. Here are some suggestions for those who would be solo puppeteers.

Keep everything as simple as possible.

The ideal one-person show has only two or three characters, one setting, and no props. Of course, this eliminates about 90 percent of all the stories you might want to adapt, so you need to be creative. As we saw in the last chapter, "The Three Little Pigs" can be adapted easily if you are willing to play with the story a bit. The more props, puppets, and scenery pieces you have, the more things can go wrong. Cultivate the virtues of simplicity and clarity. The younger the children in your audience, the fewer "fussy" details you should include. Your scenery pieces and props should include only what's absolutely necessary. A single bed can represent a bedroom; a single desk with a small sign reading "Hotel" or "Library" can stand for those places.

Props should be larger than life in proportion to the puppets and easy for the puppets to handle. The three-year-old in the last row should be able to see that Little Red Riding Hood is carrying a basket. To accomplish that, the basket may need to be almost as large as Little Red.

Action and wit cover a multitude of problems.

Plan each story and each scene as a sequence of actions that logically follow one another. Always know your characters well enough to anticipate how each will walk, talk, jump, or otherwise react in any situation you place them into. Familiarity with your characters will help you if anything goes wrong. If a prop falls off the playboard, if you are suddenly consumed by the urge to sneeze, or if a puppet gets hooked on a piece of scenery, don't "ignore" it. Have your puppet—in character—ask someone in the front row to please hand him the prop. (The children are almost always very anxious to help.) Have one of your characters sneeze and the other puppet onstage say "Gesundheit." Have another character—even if you have to bring the other character onstage for just this purpose—help the puppet who is hooked on the scenery detach herself, and then *go right on* as if it's no big deal.

If you don't break character or grind the show to a halt—two of the biggest no-nos there are in theatrical performances of any kind—the audience will usually think it's part of the show. If you like to improvise, you can even add a little flourish to mishaps. For example, after your Troll in "The Three Billy Goats Gruff" sneezes because you have to sneeze, he might say, "Hoo boy! That's what comes from living under a bridge." Then go on with the show.

**Don't be afraid to improvise, but gear
it to your audience.**

Improvisation is one of the delights of solo puppetry. If you are performing in a school, for example, you might have the Wolf say to Little Red Riding Hood,

I know a shortcut to Grandma's house. Just go that way (*pointing with his nose*), turn left at Ms. Wilson's room, and go past the monkey bars.

Audiences love being in on a joke, particularly one that refers to people, places, or things they know personally.

Be sure that the audience will get your jokes, though. As much as I love bad puns, I never use them when my audience is younger than the fourth grade because most younger children lack the verbal skills to appreciate them. On the other hand, children as young as kindergarten seem to love knock-knock jokes, though, whether they get them or not.

Plan your sequence of events, your scene changes, and the locations of your puppets very carefully.

Performing a solo puppet show is like singing and playing the piano while simultaneously reading the music and watching the audience's reaction: Your brain, eyes, voice, and body are all very busy, and each must do its job at exactly the right second. Most of us wouldn't dream of doing it all without first practicing a lot in private. Before your first rehearsal of a new show, picture the stage from the audience's point of view.

Which character enters first?

How does she enter?

From which side does she enter?

What happens next?

Who enters next, and from where?

Go through the entire show in your mind and block it out, considering every entrance and exit, scenery change, sound effect, prop, and puppet change. Plan something for the hero to do onstage while the comic assistant goes off to get the magic wand. Plan enough time to flash the lights during the magical transformation into a pumpkin.

When you're through blocking it out, plan carefully where everything will go backstage so you'll be able to grab anything within five seconds if necessary. Once you have all the puppets, props, scenery pieces, and special effects in place in your mind, set them up in reality and run through the show. The amount of time it takes to make even a simple change of puppets or scenery may surprise you, but if you've kept everything simple, you'll train yourself to work wonders swiftly.

Never, never, *never* read from a script as you perform, and never perform to a tape of the script.

Although I compared solo puppetry to playing a piano, you should never "read your music" as you perform. Puppetry is like storytelling—you must be familiar and comfortable with the story you're presenting before you begin. You don't need to have every word memorized unless you're presenting a song or a poem, but you do need to know the "message" of the story, its mood, the sequence of events, the rise and fall of the plot, and any catch phrases that will repeat through the story, such as "Little Pig, Little Pig, let me come in." "No! Not by the hair of my chinny-chin-chin!"

If you feel the need to know every line by heart, and you can't take time to memorize every line, you will be tempted to tape up the script inside the stage and read it as you manipulate the puppets. *Don't.* A solo puppeteer has too many other things to be concerned about backstage—remembering where a certain prop is, being aware of where the puppet's eyes are looking, and finding the next puppet in time for her entrance. All these concerns will make you look away from the script, and everything will stop onstage while you find your place on the script. Even if you don't lose your place, you will be concentrating so hard on reading that you will not be watching where a puppet's eyes are looking or even whether his mouth is moving, and the show will lose believability. When you perform you are a part of a triangle that consists of you, the puppets, and the audience, and you must never allow anything to break off one—or two—of the triangle's sides by distracting your attention.

One of the virtues of solo puppetry is that every show can be at least a little different from all the others. Since you don't need to worry about messing up another performer's cues, you don't need to worry about following a written script slavishly. If you need help learning your lines, read the script onto an audiocassette and play it in your car while you're driving, on your Walkman while you ride the bus, or at home while you're dusting or gardening. I always read my scripts aloud three times and then set them aside. If you do something similar, your shows will be both livelier and more lifelike.

When you play that tape, don't manipulate the puppets to it. Instead, learn the story and then perform both the actions and voices live. If you put the lines on tape because you feel you're not loud enough, work on your voice exercises (see chapter 2) or get yourself a microphone and a portable sound system, such as a karaoke box. No matter how well a script has been read and recorded, a tape is still a tape. One of the virtues of live performance is that it's not like 99 percent of entertainment a child sees.

Tape players are just one more thing that goes wrong when you least expect it. If you use one at all, use it for background or preshow music only, and be sure to use a good-sized boom box with decent bass.

Always have something happening on stage.
Never have your puppets just standing there talking. They should always be doing something, be preparing to do something, or have just done something. Most of today's young children have grown up in front of

television sets and usually have very little experience as audience members at a live performance. They expect nonstop high-speed action and have little patience with an empty, quiet puppet stage. Many library and school puppet shows performed by volunteers or staff feature long scene changes every few minutes, usually while a little cassette recorder plays music tinnily in the background. The story stops dead, the curtain closes, the puppeteers are frantically pulling scenery pieces on and off and changing puppets, and the audience's attention is wandering all over the room. When the curtain opens on the next scene, it takes a minute or two to settle the audience again, and the flow of the story is jumbled.

Smart solo puppeteers, having worked out every detail of each character's entrances and exits, will still find themselves wishing for four hands when it's time for a scene change or a magical transformation. If the stage remains bare for more than thirty seconds—and thirty seconds is a *very* long time for a TV-trained child—your change is taking too long. There are two good ways to get yourself through these tricky spots. First, if a character must exit to allow you to have two hands free to change his clothes, put on another puppet, switch your puppet from one hand to the other, or execute a magical transformation and continue speaking as that character. For example, if the puppet is in the midst of changing from a frog to a prince, he can vanish from the stage but the audience hears him saying,

"Ohh . . . what's happening to me? My legs are getting longer . . . I'm standing up straight . . . **I'm not green anymore!**"

Then he reappears transformed—or more accurately, the frog puppet is set aside backstage and the prince puppet enters. If a puppet is being switched from one hand to another (luckily, this doesn't need to be done very often), he can be talking to the children about looking for something (or someone, depending on the script) backstage. Dialogue can also go on behind the curtain during a scene change, and if you know your characters well, it can be improvised to any length desired.

The best way for a solo puppeteer to change scenery is to have the puppets change it themselves in full view of the audience. By not closing the curtain and stopping the story, you can take your time about it, even make a show out of it. For years I have performed a double-bill show of "The Gingerbread Boy" and "The Three Billy Goats Gruff" and tied the show together with a puppet master of ceremonies. Between the two shows, the emcee removes a bush, moves the river, and places the bridge onstage, all the while prattling on about the show and complaining that he has to move all this heavy scenery by himself. He even trips and falls with one scenery piece as I rattle a box of odd metal parts with my foot backstage; it sounds like everything backstage has fallen over. It keeps up the personal joke between the puppets and the audience that "it's all just a show," and it rarely fails to get a laugh from the children.

Working with Another Puppeteer

Even the most confirmed solo puppeteer shouldn't pass up occasional opportunities to perform with others. However, even if you're working with a second person, you both don't need to be puppeteers the whole time. Be creative with your bodies and your presences. For some shows, one of you can come out in front with a guitar, autoharp, or other instrument and teach the puppet worked by the second performer a silly song, and the puppet keeps making silly mistakes. (Try a song that's easy to mess up, like "Hole in the Bottom of the Sea" or "The Cat Went Fiddle-I-Fee.") The performer outside the stage can put on a costume (or bits of a costume) and be a witch, princess, or other human character interacting with an animal or legendary creature puppet on the stage, or (always fun) the performer in front of the stage can be a giant interacting with a small human-character puppet. The performer outside the stage can also become, depending on the story, a "force of nature." You can become a snowfall, a waterfall, a mountain, an earthquake, the sun or moon, or a storm—with the simplest kinds of homemade costume pieces, like a decorated paper plate held in your hand or a mountain-gray blanket thrown over your shoulders. Always be looking for unusual ways to depict the characters and events in the stories you share. A person playing the part of a storm or a mountain is something kids rarely see on television.

5

Puppets, Stages, Scenery, and Props

What's more important to a puppetry performance—the material things or the nonmaterial? The nonmaterial, of course. Beautiful puppets and expertly built stages are no more than nice things to look at for a moment if there is no performer working with them. Props, scenery, stages, and puppets are really only *sort of* important, and they certainly shouldn't be your focuses. Don't sweat these things so much. Save your sweat for your characterizations, your voices, your manipulation skills, and your story.

Puppets

When most people think of puppetry, they think first of the puppets themselves—creatures of cloth, wood, plastic, cardboard, or papier mâché. This is logical; after all, during a show, the puppets are the centers of attention. Most beginners often spend more than three-quarters of the time they have to create a show on simply building and costuming the puppets.

Puppet-making is labor-intensive; if you want to perform with attractive, well-made puppets, you need to spend a lot of time making them. However, the proportion of time that goes into building them does not reflect their value to your performance as a whole. Actually, the puppets themselves are the least important part of any performance. The most important aspects include the characterizations, the voices and manipulation, and the story you want to share. If you have something to say and can say it well, you can perform a wonderful show with paper-bag puppets or Styrofoam balls on sticks. On the other hand, your audience will quickly lose interest in a show featuring beautifully crafted and costumed puppets that have little to say or do and that cannot convince the audience, for that short time, that they are alive. Therefore, concentrate your energies on your performance skills.

However, the puppets still must be made, for you will rarely happen into a store that is selling a complete set of puppets for "The Three Billy Goats Gruff," bridge included, for just $17.95! You have several choices: you can make a set of puppets yourself, have them made especially for you by a craftsperson, or buy them in a store. Each has advantages and disadvantages.

If you make your own puppets, you must find patterns, buy the cloth or other materials, and do all the work of construction. (See the sources and resources in appendix C for some places to begin your search. It always takes two to three times as long as you think it will.) However, when you're through, you will have sharpened your craft skills, created a set of puppets that are distinctly yours, and made certain that their sizes and styles will match each other. All this you will have achieved at a fairly low monetary cost but at a high cost in your time.

If a craftsperson makes the puppets, you will need to find a person with whom you can work and who understands exactly what you want and how you're going to use the puppets. You will have to approve the materials and pray that they're finished on time to rehearse. However, if you've selected the right person, you will also have a beautifully made set of puppets that will last you many years, fit you and your needs, and match one another. This you will have achieved at a fairly low cost in time but at a high cost in cash.

If you buy the puppets in a store, you must first find a store or catalog that has the puppets you need. Unless you're lucky enough to find a whole set for a particular show, they probably won't match in size or style, may not fit your hand properly (most puppets you buy in stores are sized for children's hands, not adults'), and may vary widely in quality. The main advantages of buying puppets are that you don't have to do the work yourself, and you need to spend only a moderate amount of money.

What to Look for in a Puppet

If your school or library has a collection of odd puppets lying around, you can often be creative, and add a few details that will transform them into your needed characters. An old man puppet can be changed into a king or a miller, or a young woman into a princess or witch, with the right headgear and cloak. Animal figures are more difficult to alter without altering them permanently, but a frog can be temporarily turned into a grasshopper by adding pipe-cleaner antennae and a winglike cape, and a rat puppet can be changed to a possum simply by calling him one in the show. However, you probably will need to purchase puppets from a catalog or a toy store, construct puppets, or supervise construction of puppets for some shows you want to perform. When you do, here is what to look for in a good performance puppet:

Be aware of the eyes.
In chapter 2 you learned that the audience looks where the puppet looks and that the puppeteer should always control where the puppet is looking. Especially with young children, the eyes are the places your audience "reads" your character's movements, so be sure that the eyes are large and easy to see across the room. Most "toy" puppets you can buy in stores have small dark plastic eyes that are used in teddy bears and other stuffed animals. When mounted in a head made of fake fur material, such eyes are often buried in the fur and hard to make out. Many cute store-bought animal puppets become mere balls of fur on a puppet stage. Most professional puppets, on the other hand, have large white eyes with black pupils that can be seen from the last row. Note the difference in the eyes of the puppets shown in figure 5.1. Toy puppets, like the teddy bear on the left, are intended for individual play, not for performing for a large audience. If you have some toy puppets that you'd like to use for a performance, make some larger eyes for them from felt and paste them on. The children will find them easier to "focus" on.

**Be certain the puppets are loose enough
to perform a wide range of movements,
yet easy to control.**
Because most toy puppets are made for children, they are often too tight on adult hands. If you can "let them out" a bit, do so. When trying out a puppet in a store, run it through a wide range of motions.

Will a glove puppet be able to wave both arms?

Can it pick up objects of various sizes?

Can you make it clap its hands?

■ **FIGURE 5.1** Standard and Enhanced Eyes for Puppets

SMALL "TEDDY BEAR"
EYES

LARGE "PUPPET"
EYES

Is it easy to make it bend over and bow?

Will a mouth puppet be able to make faces?

Can a mouth puppet open and close its mouth around syllables of various sizes?

Is it easy to pick up props with the mouth puppet?

When you twist a mouth puppet's neck around, does it bind?

An uncomfortably tight puppet means a puppeteer who will not be able to concentrate as well on performing. A puppet that is too large, loose, or floppy is equally difficult to use. If it's too loose, get some polyester pillow stuffing or half-inch sheets of foam rubber to stuff into the loose areas around your fingers. This is especially for mouth puppets, which must be snug enough to be able to "speak" properly. There's nothing more unnerving than a loose mouth puppet that looks as if it's chewing on its toothless gums instead of moving its mouth crisply.

Make sure all the puppets in a particular show are in scale to, and in style with, one another.

If most of the hand puppets are basically the same size, the Lion and the Mouse, for example, might be exactly the same height. If you're performing the Aesop's fable by that name, much of its impact is lost. To give "The Three Billy Goats Gruff" the proper impact, the Troll needs to bulk visibly larger than the Little Billy Goat Gruff. Mouth puppets are easier to make larger or smaller by having them fit almost as snugly as gloves or bulking out their bodies with a layer of half-inch foam rubber. Very small characters, like insects or mice, who need to interact with much larger creatures should be stick puppets controlled from below. For example, the mouse in my version of "The Three Little Pigs" (see appendix A) is a stick puppet made from the same fake-fur material as the Wolf puppet. This reinforces the important comparison in sizes between the old Wolf and the new Mouse. (See figure 5.2 for a comparison of these proportions.) The transformation from Wolf to Mouse needs to be made quickly, and having the Mouse as a stick puppet makes it easy to snatch up immediately after the Wolf has vanished from view. In this play, the quicker the switch, the more impressive the change in size appears. The stick Mouse is also fun to play for laughs. Because he's basically a little stuffed animal on a stick, I can make him jump around nervously and spin around as he looks for a way to escape.

Also be careful that your puppets match one another stylistically. The King should not be a glove puppet with a Styrofoam ball for its head while the Queen is a velour mouth puppet. If all the puppets in a set—like all your Billy Goats Gruff or all three of your Little Pigs—are made of the same materials and made with an equal attention to detail, your characters will be more believable and easier to see as "real."

STICK
PUPPET
MOUSE
(3" LONG)

MOUTH
PUPPET
WOLF
(15" HIGH)

**Be certain your puppets can do what you
need them to do.**

Handling props is always a tricky business. Even if you rehearse diligently, the time will come when a prop will fall off the stage. These unfortunate occasions can be minimized, though. When designing or selecting a puppet, have your props on hand to make sure the puppet can manipulate them comfortably. Most, if not all, of your human puppets should be glove puppets if they are going to be handling many props; it does not look very good if your mouth-puppet Goldilocks sticks her face in the bowl like a dog when she tastes the porridge, although it could be funny if accompanied by a slobbery noise in a slapstick version of the story. If your performance allows you to use both your hands to work a single puppet, you can supply a mouth puppet with long arms moved by rods to make a hand-and-rod puppet. (See figure 5.3.)

Hand-and-rod puppets make your human (and some animal and monster) mouth puppets much more lifelike. But unless you put small wire hooks on each prop or Velcro on both the hand and the prop, they won't be any more able to handle things than those without rods. For making gestures, however, hand-and-rod puppets are superb; it just takes a while

■ **FIGURE 5.3** Hand-and-Rod Puppet Example

COAT-HANGER
WIRE INSERTED
INTO HOLES IN
UNDERSIDES OF
WRISTS

LOOP
INSERTED
INTO CLOTH
HAND

to learn to master holding both rod handles in the same hand and making convincing gestures. It's a lot like learning to use chopsticks. When working with a hand-and-rod puppet, the temptation is to let one arm just hang and gesture with the other, but for realism, both arms should move at least a little. If you have difficulty working both rods, remove the rod from the less-used arm and tie about four inches of clear fishing line to the bottom of the puppet's neck and the upper part of its wrist so its arm will sway as if bent, moving as the puppet moves.

Stages and "Nonstages"

It isn't necessary to use a stage to perform with a puppet. However, audiences seem to like shows with stages best, probably because stages hide the puppeteer's body and promote the idea that the little creatures on the stage really *are* alive. Most puppeteers prefer to work behind a stage as well. Appendix B provides plans for two traveling stages that have worked well when performing for audiences of young children.

There are as many kinds of hand puppet stages as there are puppeteers, but there are several basic designs to consider, depending on your performance style. These include the over-the-head stage, closed proscenium stage, and open proscenium stage. (See figure 5.4.)

You will notice that the stage plans in appendix B are stages in which the puppeteer performs standing, not sitting. I believe that if you want to perform the best show you are able to, you should perform standing. A good puppet show needs tension, energy, and flexibility; when you sit through

■ **FIGURE 5.4**   Three Basic Designs for Puppet Stages

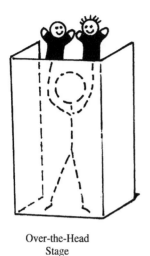
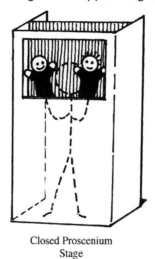

Over-the-Head   Closed Proscenium   Open Proscenium
    Stage   Stage   Stage

the show, your body becomes "fixed" in one spot. It becomes harder to have puppets run, jump, chase, and hide from this position. In contrast, you can turn, bend, reach high, and bounce up and down on your feet when you perform standing. A "perform-while-standing" stage is also taller, of course, which means your audience can see the performance area better. (Of course, some talented puppeteers perform from wheelchairs and offer outstanding performances from a sitting position.)

Over-the-Head Stage

The over-the-head stage is rarely seen among nonprofessional puppeteers because most of them feel uncomfortable performing with their arms above their heads for long periods of time. However, this classic Punch-and-Judy design has a number of real advantages. If you have an audience of more than fifty people, they will have a much easier time seeing what's going on onstage because the stage is so tall. In addition, it's easier to keep the puppets on a constant performance level because you're holding them steadily overhead. By turning around inside the stage, you will also be able to make your puppets enter from either side of the stage or chase each other in a circle. If more than one puppeteer is working inside the stage, they'll be able to walk around each other, giving all puppets equal access to all parts of the performance area.

Closed Proscenium Stage

A closed proscenium stage allows you to perform either standing or sitting within a stage opening like a TV screen. A puppeteer who performs standing, as I recommend, will be able to utilize not only the playboard (stage "floor") as a performance area but the top and sides of the stage as well, as shown in figure 5.5. The proscenium is the stage opening. This style has both a backdrop curtain, or scrim, that covers your face and a curtain that can be closed before and after the performance and during scene changes. The advantage of this style is both being able to see through the scrim to know what is happening onstage and having the front curtain, if this is what you want. I don't recommend a front curtain for shows with audiences under eight years old because I dislike long scene changes with the curtain closed, but many puppeteers wouldn't have their stage any other way.

Open Proscenium Stage

The open proscenium stage can be used either standing or sitting, but it eliminates the front curtain and the TV-screen-like opening in favor of an open stage without sides. On this type of stage all scene changes must be done before the audience. This is the type of stage I have used for years. I like it because I am forced to keep something going onstage at all times and because I can use the top of the background curtain as a "second stage." For example, in "The Three Little Pigs" during the chase between the Second Little Pig and the Wolf, both characters take turns appearing "upstairs" while the other is "downstairs" on the playboard, and they switch positions rapidly. This style of stage also allows audience members seated on either side of the stage a better view.

■ **FIGURE 5.5**   Parts of a Closed Proscenium Puppet Stage

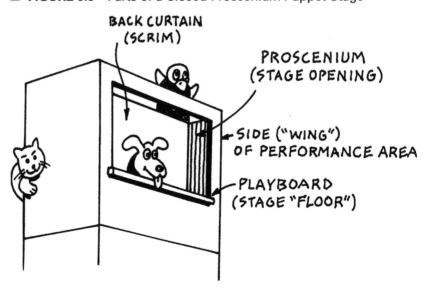

Factors in Choosing a Stage

Regardless of the type of stage you use, keep the following principles in mind.

How portable and sturdy is the stage?

If a stage is meant to travel or is intended to be up only during rehearsals and performances, it should be light, easily transported from one location to another, and easy to set up and take down. Professional puppeteers often use large, elaborate stages with metal frames and velvet curtains that take up to two hours to erect. A librarian/puppeteer can rarely take this sort of time.

If a stage is meant to travel, it should have a frame of light wood, PVC pipe, or similar material and a cloth cover. Solid wood stages are usually tremendously awkward and heavy if they have to be moved. One library received a bequest for a puppet stage for its children's room; the stage was intended to be used for special performances only. The head librarian, knowing nothing about puppet stages but wanting something impressive, hired a carpenter who created a beautiful solid hardwood folding stage weighing more than one hundred pounds and completely impractical for actual performances.

What impression does the stage make on the audience? Does the stage compete with the puppets?

Although it is natural to want a stage that gives the audience a warm, happy, expectant feeling, it is easy to create a stage that overwhelms the puppets instead. If a stage is bright red, orange, or yellow, it will attract the audience's eyes constantly during a performance and literally steal the show from the puppets. This point goes double for stages made in the shapes of circus tents, castles, elephants, or anything else. The ideal stage should be simply shaped and covered with material in cool colors. The *show* should be showy, not the stage. Many stages are covered with black material; however, blue, green, or violet fabric with vertical stripes gives a pleasant, festive air without being overpowering.

The stage must be comfortable for you, or nothing else matters.

While standing or (ahem) sitting, you must be able to reach all the puppets, props, scenery pieces, and switches or sound effects you'll need to perform your show. Don't put yourself in the position of having to stretch from a standing position to pick a prop up from the floor while working a puppet with the other hand.

Puppets should hang at about waist height and allow you to slip your hands in and out easily. A prop shelf about one to two feet below the playboard provides a place from which all the necessary props can be

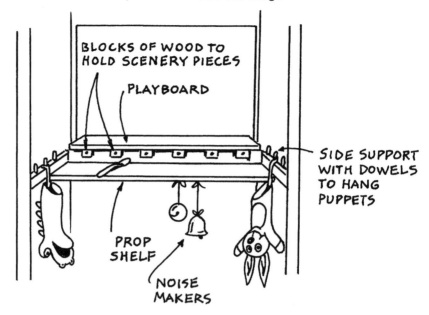

■ **FIGURE 5.6** Prop Holders inside the Stage

BLOCKS OF WOOD TO
HOLD SCENERY PIECES

PLAYBOARD

SIDE SUPPORT
WITH DOWELS
TO HANG
PUPPETS

PROP
SHELF

NOISE
MAKERS

grabbed quickly and scenery pieces can be hung. Figure 5.6 shows a rear view of a closed proscenium stage during a show, with puppets hanging upside down and ready to slip one's hands into, noisemakers hanging inside from the prop shelf, and a prop on the prop shelf. The playboard should be at a reasonable and comfortable height. You shouldn't need to perform on your knees or in a crouch or on your tiptoes. If you are performing with another person, is there enough room for both of you? Can both of you reach everything that needs to be reached?

Nonstages

It isn't always necessary to use a big-enough-to-cover-your-body stage to perform with puppets, however. For casual performances and storytelling with puppets, several kinds of "nonstages" work well. Throw a sheet over a pole, rest the pole on two bookstacks, and stand behind it to work the puppets and narrate. A table turned on its side may also work. A big cardboard box can be made into a train, a plane, or a house in which your puppets can perform, with you standing or sitting behind. Be aware, however, that such casual stages have no playboard and aren't set up to handle props or scenery pieces without some customizing. In performance situations like these, go out of your way to wink, metaphorically speaking, at the kids in the audience. The story should be told in a light-hearted, relaxed fashion, encouraging audience participation and impressing on the children your love of the story. When all is said and done, the stage doesn't matter; the performance does.

Simple Scenery and Props

Many beginning puppeteers seem to believe that a puppet show must have elaborate scenery and props to be worthwhile. Some are willing to sacrifice their rehearsal time, the pacing of a show, and the attention spans of their audience members to close the curtains and fuss with the ornate thrones, backdrops, mountains, and castles they have spent hours sewing, painting, or building.

Scenery

While complex scenery can add a lot to shows for older children and adults, not only is "big" scenery not necessary for performances for young children but it can get in the way of their enjoyment of a show. The younger a child is, the more his or her eyes are constantly moving, soaking in every detail of the environment. A young child expends plenty of mental energy simply following a story. Detailed scenery (much like an elaborate, brightly colored puppet stage) drains away some of this energy. Do your audience and yourself a favor and keep things simple.

For example, a single tree can suggest a forest, particularly if the lead puppets act *with* the tree. Red Riding Hood and the Wolf should lean on the tree, cower behind the tree, peek and sneak around the tree, and use it to get the message across that they're in a deep, dark forest. In "The Magic Knapsack" (in appendix A), a single object often suggests what could be an elaborate scene: a fireplace is a hotel room and a desk with a sign reading "Ritz Hotel" is a hotel lobby. Coupled with a script that tells the audience where the action is taking place, such simple scenery not only leaves the puppeteer free to concentrate on the acting but leaves the young child in the audience free to concentrate on the story and to fill in the blanks with his or her imagination.

Build simple scenery pieces from sturdy materials, in easy-to-identify shapes, and in basic primary and secondary colors. Think of each scenery piece as a symbol for something rather than an actual object. Don't bother painting in each brick of your Third Pig's house or of your castle; three flowers, not twenty, are all that's needed to suggest a flowerbed. Look at the illustrations in the most popular picture books; backgrounds are usually simply drawn and colored, without intricate and fussy detail. In my experience, young children seem to take more naturally to the simplicity of Anne Rockwell, Tomie dePaola, and Frank Asch than the beautiful complexity of Chris Van Allsburg and Trina Schart Hyman, who appeal more to older children and adults. When designing and building your scenery, look at the first three illustrators' books for inspiration.

Attaching scenery to your stage quickly and securely and then removing it quickly for scene changes will always be a pain. Either you must close the curtains and have your audience stare at nothing for a minute or two or

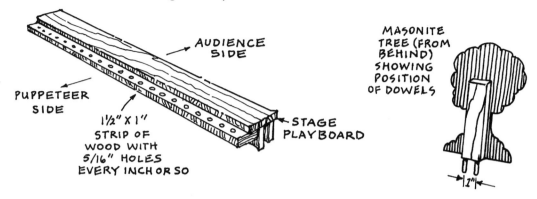

■ **FIGURE 5.7** Dowel Peg Scenery Holder

AUDIENCE SIDE

PUPPETEER SIDE

1½" X 1" STRIP OF WOOD WITH 5/16" HOLES EVERY INCH OR SO

STAGE PLAYBOARD

MASONITE TREE (FROM BEHIND) SHOWING POSITION OF DOWELS

2"

your puppets must change the scenery onstage, which is often like trying to unlock a door while holding a tennis ball in each hand and wearing gloves. There are several possibilities worth investigating, however, such as adding a wooden strip with dowel holes at one- or two-inch intervals that allow props and scenery pieces to be made with ¼" dowel pegs on the bottom. (See figure 5.7.) The dowel pegs allow the puppets to set up their own scenery easily.

If scenery will remain on the stage throughout the performance, scenery pieces can be tied to the sides with pipe cleaners that are glued into the scenery, or they can be hooked over the top of the proscenium arch with bent black wire that is attached to the scenery pieces.

Props and How to Avoid Them

Take it from me, you want to mess with props as little as possible, especially if you are a one-person show. With puppets on your hands, props are difficult to pick up and handle believably. Most glove puppets look like they're picking up props with their arms or wrists instead of their hands, and mouth puppets must handle everything with their mouths, of course. (Note: When your mouth puppet animals pick up props but must say lines, are you pressing your lips together while speaking as if you were holding an object in your mouth, too? If not, you should be.)

Before including a prop in a show, ask yourself: "Is this thing really necessary?" Eliminate it if it isn't. Some props, however, like Red Riding Hood's basket—because the audience will ask you where it is if she's not carrying it—are essential. Here are my main "prop-ositions" when you're finding or making things for your puppets to use onstage.

Some props can be puppets themselves.

If a puppet character must handle an oddly shaped prop, such as a huge banana or some such (don't laugh; there are stories in which a huge banana is the correct thing for your puppet to be wrangling), consider working the prop with a free hand. I once did a show based on a Brazilian folktale in which a monkey sneaked into an enchanted garden to steal fruit, and when he tried to grab each berry or (yes) banana, it leaped away from him. I only had to work two puppets at a time in this scene—the monkey and each piece of fruit (and I mounted each piece of fruit on a dowel).

If you're doing a comic show, make your props BIG.

If, for example, you're doing a silly show in which a character must use a telephone, simply use a "dead" phone from your attic or buy a toy phone. Although it's not in scale with the puppets, the children accept it—and they can see what it is much better.

If a prop must be set on the stage, make certain it's secure, yet can be removed easily.

If you can drill holes in the bottoms of props that must be fixed in place (like the telephone above) and glue a piece of dowel in the bottom of each one, you can have your puppets "plug" them into the playboard and pull them out and carry them away when no longer needed.

If some props are hard to grasp, glue or sew easy-to-hide cloth tabs on them.

The tabs give the puppet something to grasp. You could also put small pieces of Velcro on your puppets' wrists, so they can pick up things and hold them more securely.

Practice, practice, practice.

Make absolutely certain, for example, that when your hero needs to pick up his sword and threaten the dragon he can always grab it pointing in the right direction.

Make sure your props will last as long as you need them.

Puppets are rough on paper items, glass items, and anything else breakable or crushable. They tend to drop things and grab them a little too hard. Plastic items (such as artificial fruit and flowers and some toys) make better props than those of more organic heritage.

As with everything else in this book, use your imagination, cruise the junk shops, and be creative with what you find. As long as you believe in your performance, your props need not be slavishly realistic or expensive.

6

Puppetry as Part of Your Job

No matter how much time you spend building your puppets, how many times you rehearse your show, and how comfortable you are with your characters, you have to perform in front of a real group of children. You must perform before them in a particular room, usually in a particular library or school. Performing on a regular basis before children is a joy most of the time, as long as you're careful to prepare yourself for things that might go wrong. If you're not, occasional nightmares can pop out when you're not ready for them.

Know Your Audience

You must know who will be in your audience and plan the show for them. If you have been working in a particular library for a while, you should have a good idea of the age and audience skills of the children who usually attend special programs. You probably know a lot of them by name. If you work in a school, you may know almost everyone in your audience by name. In a public library situation there's a little more chance involved in who will attend.

For example, in the fifteen branches of Multnomah County Library in Portland, Oregon, in which I did much of my performing, my audiences were usually children between the ages of two and seven or eight, with the majority of the group between ages three and five. Because most of the children who attended the shows were preschoolers, I didn't use much verbal humor in my shows; I needed to stick to visual slapstick and simple plots without much subtlety. Although I occasionally threw in a joke for the older children or adults, the majority of the shows consisted of simple dialogue and lots of action on the silliest and most basic level. This means I used many variations of puppet peek-a-boo (with the villain sneaking up behind the hero and ducking out of sight when the hero turns around) and often had characters chase each other back and forth along the playboard. These actions were woven around the plot of an uncomplicated or familiar story that had simple, repetitive dialogue. If you perform for school-age children, your shows should still stress the visual, but you can add lots more verbal humor and present more stories from other times and cultures.

It's up to you to know and prepare for the audience you will get—not the audience you wish you had. You will need to customize your show for your audience and not expect your audience to adjust to your show. Sometimes hired or volunteer performers who are used to playing before school-age audiences present a very verbal, artistic show to an audience of preschoolers and wonder why the audience gets restless and begins responding inappropriately.

Don't expect an audience of young children to behave "properly." One of your tasks as a children's librarian is to encourage the children attending your programs to learn good audience skills. Remember, most modern children are used to sitting in front of a video screen that demands nothing of them. Unless an adult tells them to do so, for example, they often don't applaud. Even with a big climax, they're sometimes not sure that the show has ended; they get their cues from Mom or their preschool teacher. When I use Artie, my "master of ceremonies" noodlehead character, in a show, he often comes out at the end, waves at the kids, and says, "That's all! It's over! Goodbye! See you later . . . and don't forget to take some books home with you!"

Performing for young children should give both performer and audience a sense of freedom. However, because young children usually haven't learned what behavior is expected of them as audience members, freedom without guidance can lead to chaos. Therefore, you must explain before the beginning of your performance how you expect the children to behave as good audience members, and you can do it easily without being forbidding.

Performing in a Library

Following are a few recommendations for managing a puppet show in a library. These are based on experiences in about two thousand shows over seventeen years in more than one hundred libraries. The examples emphasize problems faced performing in public libraries because although they happen rarely, they *do* happen. Few books on puppetry tell you what to do about them. Marie Noe of the Abilene, Texas, Public Library gave me a gem of advice about performing in a library situation: "Always, *always,* **always** have a back-up plan."

Children need guidelines in new and different situations. Because puppet shows in libraries are unusual situations for most children, setting guidelines for behavior—without overemphasizing them—makes a show more fun for everyone. Often it's not necessary to state guidelines at all. Simply setting up the room and doing a little preparation takes care of many problems that could arise.

Space Limitations

Part of the library puppeteer's need to set guidelines comes from having to perform in a space that was never designed to be a performance space. A few large libraries have real theaters with fixed seats, and many others have small auditoriums or meeting rooms. However, at least half of the shows I've done have been presented in the middle of a library's children's area. Tables are shoved against the walls, carpet squares are thrown on the floor in front of the puppet stage, and chairs are arranged in semicircles to seat the adults farther away. Unless your library is blessed with a large area for the performance, do not place any chairs closer than twenty feet to the stage. Joking about the fire marshal aside, you can fit a lot more young people on an empty expanse of floor than you can in chairs.

Frequently, particularly if the exit is on one side of the performance area, groups of children and parents will "bunch up" around the exit. This leaves a lot of empty space at the far side of the audience area. Parents of young children often want to be able to leave quickly, and they don't want to haul their little ones over a sea of children. However, if a big crowd attends, it's time to do "the scoot." When this happens, point to the empty area and say something like, "We've got lots of space over here, and everyone's sitting over *there*. So I need everyone to scoot this way until you bump into the person next to you. Come on, scoot! Scoot! Scoot!" I make a rhythmic scooting motion, moving my tush and my arms aerobically in the direction I want the audience to move. Now, many of the parents and older children like the place they're sitting just fine and don't want to move. So (and here is the important part) I *just keep scooting* until everyone gets the point that the show won't start until they scoot, and they move enough to let everyone find a place to sit down.

The stage itself usually sits in front of bookshelves or a window, almost never a blank wall. While this sort of free-form audience space can work well for a clown, a singer, a magician, or a storyteller, it sometimes causes problems for a puppeteer who isn't actually seen as he or she performs. This presents a problem because if there is no adult to prevent it, children may sneak around and watch you perform from behind. (One puppeteer had such a child actually enter the back of the stage unasked and unwanted and begin handling the puppets and props while the child's parent sat in the audience with an "Isn't he cute?" smile.) Toddlers particularly, who are used to lots of individual attention and want to handle everything, are prone to wander behind puppet stages. Therefore, you'll probably want to use a bottler. (This function is described fully in the following section.)

As previously mentioned, preschoolers rarely applaud without an adult to cue them. They stand up in front of the other children to see better, not realizing they're blocking other children's views. They don't quite understand how to respond properly in a group situation to the dialogue and action. These and other behavior problems come with the territory. You must have in mind how you will deal with them when they arise.

You must also deal with the fact that some parents are sorely tempted to drop their children in the children's area for half an hour and go over to browse the new fiction area or research VCRs in *Consumer Reports*. Others may run in to find out how long the show is, then rush off to the market or the dry cleaner's. Fortunately, *most* of the children left in the library know how to behave, but having so many of them in the building at once can cause problems. Be vigilant and make sure other trustworthy eyes are watching what is going on.

In many preschool audiences, a child will continuously shout, "You're *silly*," or something similar, to one of the puppets, expecting a response, while other children are trying to hear the dialogue. I ignore it and go on with the show, and eventually the child will stop. When you're used to giving preschool children encouragement, it's not easy to suddenly ignore them. However, in this case the performance and all the other children in the audience require that you ignore one child's behavior.

One solution to keeping children from behind the stage is to set up a "puppeteer-only" area for the duration of your show. The simplest and best way to do this is setting up what I jokingly call "the line of death" with masking tape on the floor about three feet in front of the stage. (See figure 6.1.) You probably won't want to call it this, but it fits my performance style; I facetiously tell the children: "You cross this and you die." There's always some wiseacre six-year-old who immediately crosses it, and then goes back to sit down. However, the children get the point. Most children ages three and over seem to sense instinctively that they are not to cross the tape. Toddlers are the exception, and they should have a parent, caregiver, or older sibling nearby to corral them if they feel the need to wander.

Children who are potential troublemakers, whether toddlers or twelve-year-olds, usually make themselves known before the show. If you sense that a child in the audience might be a problem, either mention (or ask the person introducing you to mention) before the show that parents need to keep an eye on their children and make sure they don't cross the tape. Another solution to this and many of these problems is to appoint a bottler.

TAPE
"LINE OF DEATH"
(CLEAR ZONE)

3'

Saved by the Bottler

What is a bottler? Back in the nineteenth-century heyday of Punch and Judy shows, the Punch "professors" usually had an assistant called a *bottler* who had three tasks: The bottler blew a trumpet and pounded a drum, announcing the show; he collected the donations during and after the performance; and he kept children from disturbing the puppeteer during the play. Even if you don't have any roaming toddlers or silly six-year-olds who throw paper airplanes at the puppets, it is always a good idea to have a responsible older person around. This person—be it a teenager, volunteer, or staff member—will need to be your eyes and ears while you perform concealed.

If no responsible older person is available, once you are behind the stage and a day-care group of thirty children and adults enters unannounced five minutes after the performance begins and the room is already packed, who will seat them? If a two-year-old has "an accident" or suddenly gets scared of the Wolf while Mom is on the other side of the library, who will get the upset child and Mom together again? Once you are behind the stage, the show must go on; it is your duty as a performer. You must not stop for anything short of a fire or an earthquake. Have someone in the room available to do these things for you.

Controlling Chaos

If you are performing in the children's area, what is happening in the rest of the room during the performance? What if someone wants that copy of *Frog and Toad Are Friends* that is right behind the puppet stage? Is there a nearby phone, computer, or copy machine that might ring, beep, or grind away during the show? Before performances, work out with other members of the library staff how they will do their regular work while you're roaring and slaying dragons in their midst. Most library staffs are wonderfully cooperative—*if* you tell them what to do. Although it's rare to find a library user who tries to look for a book shelved directly behind your stage during your show, it doesn't hurt for the rest of your staff to know what to do about it if it happens. They might simply smile and say, "We'll help you with that right after the program."

Children in organized groups—day camps, child-care groups, YMCA groups, and others—can be downright dangerous to a carefully planned show in an open children's area. Any group of children together regularly for more than a week develops its own behavioral style and social order with leaders and followers. (Some rowdy groups of children attending my shows have brought *The Lord of the Flies* to mind.)

For example, once during a summer performance of "The Gunniwolf," in the days before I insisted on a bottler for each show, I had a couple of ringleaders in a visiting summer day-camp group decide in the middle of the show that it would be hilarious to continuously chant "Eat her! Eat her!" whenever the Gunniwolf and Little Girl were together onstage (which was most of the time). Since nothing short of stopping the show and coming out of the stage (which I won't do) will stop this kind of behavior, I went on with the show as if nothing were happening. For a short time the chanting grew so loud that nobody in the room could hear the puppets, but eventually the chanters got bored and stopped. The adults minding the group were sitting there watching the show as if nothing unusual were happening.

As another example, a pair of librarian/puppeteers once thought it would be fun during a Christmas show to throw some Styrofoam "snow" from behind the stage into the space between the stage and the audience. *Big* mistake. The children in the front row grabbed the "snow" and started throwing it at the stage and each other, whooping and giggling. Chaos ensued, and it took a while for the adults to catch on that there was a problem and get things calmed down again.

The moral of these stories is that you should not expect the adults accompanying a group always to do what *you* think they should do. These sorts of situations are very rare, but they are reasons to have a bottler who can ease over to the adults and suggest that they quiet their charges.

After the show is another potentially unpredictable time. For example, I usually bring a puppet out to meet and talk with the children after the show; my puppet dog Fred, for example, likes to come out and give each child who wants one a "slurp." (I accompany each slurp with a loud noise, and even eight- and nine-year-olds love it.) In many groups a child insists on grabbing the puppet, twisting its nose, pulling its ears, and trying to yank it off my hand. Such a child is usually overexcited and seeking attention, so I find it best to firmly grasp the child's hand with my free hand, hold the puppet up out of harm's way, and spend an extra moment interacting with that child.

Children fascinated by your show will often run up to the stage afterward and try to peek inside. Some won't just peek, they'll try to grab your puppets and play with them—roughly—even if you ask them not to. Some librarian/puppeteers don't mind if children play with their puppets after the show—usually these are people who haven't made their own puppets. Others have had the puppets they painstakingly made by hand abused by eager audience members often enough to make a point of prohibiting the children from handling the puppets and props. A good rule is "You're welcome to look, but please don't touch."

I almost always sing with the children before a show, and I once lost my favorite baritone ukelele, one I had used for hundreds of storytimes and puppetry and storytelling programs, after a successful Summer Reading Program show. There were more than 150 children and parents in the library, and at the end of the show I brought a puppet out to greet the children. Even though they knew not to cross the tape, a group of big, rowdy older boys (eight- to ten-year-olds) ran backstage and started playing—not gently—with the puppets. I asked them to please come out from behind, but they were having too good a time to listen to me. As I was about to head back and chase them out, I heard a crash, and the boys dropped the puppets and ran away. When I got behind the stage, my beloved baritone uke was on the floor, smashed beyond repair. I don't believe they smashed it deliberately; they seem to have accidentally knocked it off the bookshelf behind the stage and stepped on it. A new uke cost me eighty dollars, so I learned an expensive lesson. The library staff had all been busy dealing with the work added by simply having 150 more people in the building, and they figured I could handle the audience alone. Until I heard the crash, so did I. Since that day I've always been careful to have a bottler on hand.

Sample Program Activities

How long should a library puppet program be? If your primary audience is three- to eight-year-olds, your show by itself shouldn't be much longer than half an hour. Most young children get restless if they must sit longer than forty-five minutes, although how long they can sit often depends more on how well the show speaks to them. If you feel you need a longer program, add some singing or movement activities to fill the rest of the time.

The following format works well for solo puppetry programs:

1. Introduce yourself and (in your own library) do a "commercial" announcing upcoming library activities.
2. Begin with a song and audience participation activity (approximately five minutes long) on a theme related to that of the puppet show.
3. Tell a related story using puppets or include an audience participation story or rhyme (for a total of seven to ten minutes).
4. Present your twenty- to thirty-five-minute puppet show, for a total program of thirty-five to forty-five minutes.
5. You may want to end with another short, lighthearted song.

Other activities, such as crafts, can be added as well if you have the help. Don't add activities like crafts when you're doing everything yourself. Changing hats several times during a program—singer, storyteller, puppeteer—and then doing something as energy-intensive as a craft can be exhausting.

You can use puppets in the library in a number of ways besides doing full-length puppet shows with a stage. As mentioned in chapter 4, you can use a puppet as a storytime mascot and use groups of hand and stick puppets to tell stories. You can also use puppets to lead singing at, for example, holiday programs. If you do, however, always keep your puppet's character in your head as you perform. When a puppet sings, a puppet should sing in character. For example, my frog Henry sings in his own froggy way, in a voice and character distinct from my own, swaying back and forth and hopping around as he belts out each song.

If your library brings in other performers—magicians, storytellers, clowns, or even other puppeteers—a puppet can also assist you in hosting and introducing these programs. Work things out in advance with the other performer so your puppet can tell the performer a joke (or be the performer's foil) or be the subject or helper in one of the magician's tricks.

Puppets can also do things like pull the winning numbers in prize drawings. Mouth puppet animals work best for this, but make certain in advance that you can control them well enough to draw individual tickets out of the box.

In situations like these as well as to introduce the library to visiting child-care and classroom groups, puppets help the children focus on the presentation. The puppet can ask the children about their favorite stories or whether they have library cards or whether they'd like to hear a knock-knock joke.

FROG PUPPET:	Knock-knock.
CHILDREN:	Who's there?
FROG PUPPET:	Brig-it.
CHILDREN:	Brig-it who?
FROG PUPPET:	I want that book! Brig-it to me right now.

It's a dumb joke to adults, but children enjoy interactions with a silly sense of humor. You may want to collect silly knock-knocks and similar jokes to use in any of these kinds of "host" or "mascot" venues.

Performing Outside the Library

In these days of justifying to the public the tax money that keeps libraries running, one of the best things you can do as a children's librarian is community outreach. If you have a talent for music, storytelling, or puppets, you can be the best kind of ambassador for your library. Most preschools, child-care centers, elementary schools, community recreation facilities, and other institutions that serve children and families love having a visit from an entertainer, particularly one from a "safe" place like the library who isn't trying to sell anything (except of course reading and using the library). Few things will build better library-community relations than taking your shows out to children and families in the community.

Few librarian/puppeteers, however, have much time to get out of their buildings, particularly when they have to pack a stage, lights, and a sound system as well as puppets and props (and monthly library calendars, and library card applications, and . . .). Actually you don't need most of this stuff. I usually carry a small folding stage of PVC pipe (see appendix B) when I perform, but sometimes I just bring my baritone ukelele and a bag of puppets for singing and storytelling.

It may also be true that you, dear reader, are not on the paid library staff but are a volunteer who will be helping the regular children's services staff reach out to its community. Either way, it's important to decide on your limits and make them known to those who will be having you as a guest in their preschool, child-care center, school, or other venue.

Following are a few things to think about when representing the library by performing in the community. Your goals are to make the maximum impact on your audience, to remind them that the library's there and is pretty great, and to associate the library—and you—with a happy experience. Reaching the parents is just as important as reaching the children.

Always carry an extra story or two or have a different song ready to sing.

Have a story or song that will work when the group you're performing for turns out to be younger, older, or squirrelier than you had hoped. In other words, be prepared for a different audience than you expected.

Respect yourself 1—Don't serve as a babysitter, unless you want to.

It has been said that librarians are professional codependents—they don't know how to say "no"—and that children's librarians are the most codependent of all. Sometimes community groups and preschools holding meetings for parents will try to locate some volunteer (in this case, you) to "entertain the children" while the meetings are going on. Don't get yourself too deeply into doing this, unless you truly want to.

If you do, be sure that there will always be another adult present to speak to the children if there's a problem while you're performing, and keep those extras (from the first point) up your sleeves in case the meeting runs longer than expected. Don't undervalue your skills and value as a performer, though, and be sure to send those parents home with library program schedules, card applications, and other information.

Respect yourself 2—Your performances should be an optional part of your job, not something you *must* do.

Once you become known as a performer children enjoy, you may become very popular. Sometimes individuals or groups will call and ask you to do performances in or out of the library on particular topics, like "Mexico" or "safety" or "sea stories." This is fine, if you have the time to assemble the necessary puppets, props, songs, and stories. Once again, make sure you have placed a value on your time and skills, and don't be quick to agree to do performances on demand unless you feel the subject is one you like and can enjoy presenting.

Respect yourself 3—Only perform under conditions in which you can be at your best.

While closely related to the previous point, this point has to do with your performance environment. For example, *never* agree to perform at a carnival, a fair, or anywhere else you will need to compete against noisy games and large-motor activities. Children in these environments can't sit still and can't concentrate—and you can hardly blame them. Insist on a separate room or a spot as far as possible from the noise if you feel you must perform at such events. Puppetry and storytelling (especially storytelling) with children only work if you are the loudest thing in the room.

When you perform away from the library, make certain that everyone there knows you are *from the library*.

You may need to repeat this over and over. When you're appearing in a community festival, a group event, or at a Chapter 1 family night, you're there as an ambassador from the library. Make the time and effort you're expending worthwhile. Being out in the community these days is often essential to getting library levies and bond measures passed in a time that expects *results* from its public employees.

Unless you have a big sign next to you the whole time saying "Foozleton Public Library," the adults at the event may not know you are from the library. They may think you're somebody the school or the chamber of commerce hired. It's important to introduce yourself as "Sally Moozle from the Foozleton Public Library." Ask the crowd how many of them have library cards. Mention the library in the middle of your presentation again, and tell a library joke during the performance.

"Why did the Mummy go to the library?"

"He wanted to get all wrapped up in a good book."

Conclude by telling the audience again that you're from the library, and send them off with library calendars and card applications.

Oh—one more thing:

Remember why you're doing it.
After you've put in enormous amounts of time and effort on your performances and the local newspaper sends out a photographer to take pictures, don't be disappointed if the photo in the paper features the open-mouthed, wide-eyed faces of the children in the audience and not you or the puppets. Always keep things in perspective, and have fun!

APPENDIX A

FIVE PUPPET SHOW SCRIPTS

In this appendix are five scripts I have written/adapted for performance in the library:

- "The Three Little Pigs"
- "The Three Billy Goats Gruff"
- "Who's the Squonk?"
- "Coyote and the Galloping Rock"
- "The Magic Knapsack"

All were quite different when first set to paper. After a rehearsal, they began to change, reshaped by my own feelings about the way the lines sounded. Then, after the first performance, they had changed some more, reshaped by the audience's reactions. No two performances of any of these scripts have ever been exactly alike since. I think of them as sketches rather than fixed written works, but they are still copyrighted © 1998 by Walter Minkel. If you decide you'd like to use them for free performance in your library or school, you have my permission. Feel free to make whatever changes will make them "yours" for free performance. (You can't sell or distribute copies of the scripts, though, or perform them for profit without permission.)

The first three of these scripts are relatively easy to perform; the other two are relatively complex. All of these shows can be performed by either one or two puppeteers. I have attempted to explain any "tricky moves" you'll need to make backstage and have provided a list of the scenery, props, and puppets you'll need. Production notes about the performance and descriptions of props follow each script.

All of these shows have been performed successfully for audiences ages three to nine or so—a typical audience range for a public library program. If the audience is largely one of school-age children, improvise a little, throwing in jokes and puns as they seem appropriate. If the audience is largely one of preschoolers, strip off much of the verbal humor and concentrate on the action. There are always adults on the sidelines of a preschool performance, however, and they appreciate it when you throw in a couple of jokes for them.

In many of my performances (although in only some of these scripts) Artie, my little baldheaded "fool" who also serves as my master of ceremonies, does a short introduction. Many of the youngest audience members visit the library for shows regularly, and Artie gives them a familiar puppet they recognize and feel at home with. If you use a puppet mascot, please substitute your own.

The Three Little Pigs

Characters:

ARTIE, teaches the magic word

AARON, THE FIRST LITTLE PIG, foolish, very timid; word *wolf* throws him into terror; builds house of straw

BERNIE, THE SECOND LITTLE PIG, also foolish, loud, overconfident; hyperactive; certain the Wolf won't get *him;* builds house of sticks

CALVIN, THE THIRD LITTLE PIG, smart, happy, and self-confident; builds house of bricks

WOLF, big, strong, extremely vain, short-tempered, oily, with deep, chortling laugh

MOUSE

Props:

straw house	coat hanger
stick house	carrot
brick house	*Cat in the Hat* book
daisy	

(Artie sings to himself offstage.)

ARTIE: Ohhh . . . Who's afraid of the Big Bad Wolf, the Big Bad Wolf, the . . . *(enters, sees audience)* Oh, hey, hi! Good afternoon! We're going to tell you the story of the Three Little Pigs here in just a minute, but *(looks around and looks backstage)* nobody else is around right now, so . . . I'd like to show you a magic trick.

I checked this great magic book out of the library and read about a magic word that's never supposed to fail. Can you keep a secret? *(pauses for audience response)* Well, listen anyway. The magic word is **Wizzlewuzzlewoozle.**

Watch this now—I'm going to make a mighty oak tree appear right here *(points)* on the stage. First I'll concentrate—*(looks at the ceiling, swaying dramatically*) mmm-**MM**-mmm. Let's all say it together: wizzlewuzzlewoozle! I wish that a mighty oak tree would appear on the stage. One-two-three!

(*lights flash on and off,*

a noise like a broken video game is heard,

and finally . . . a coat hanger pops up)

Oh. That's not a mighty oak tree. (*picks up the coat hanger and throws it backstage with a crash*) Let's try again; I'm still getting the hang of this magic stuff.

Ready? Wizzlewuzzlewoozle! I wish that a mighty oak tree would appear on the stage. One-two-three! (*more lights and noise, and this time a carrot appears*)

Hmm. Well, I'm getting closer. (*pulls out the carrot and throws it backstage with a crash*) I'll save that for my lunch.

They say the third time, ahem, is the charm. Ready again? Wizzlewuzzlewoozle! I **wish** a mighty **oak tree** would appear on the stage! **One-two-three!** (*lights and noise, and a copy of* The Cat in the Hat *pops up*)

Oh, dear. I think I need more practice. (*picks up the book and carries it off saying*) We'd better get this show started. Here comes the First Little Pig. See you soon! (*exit*)

AARON: (THE FIRST LITTLE PIG)	(*enters*) Oh, dear. Oh, dear, dear, what am I going to do? (*wrings his "hands" and paces back and forth*)
	Hello, everyone. My name is Aaron; I'm the first little pig. I'm sure you've heard of my brothers and me. Our mother told us to go out into the world and make our own way. That means I'm in big trouble because I've got to find a house to live in so You-Know-Who doesn't get me.
	You know who You-Know-Who is, don't you? (*audience answers, "The Big Bad Wolf!"*)
	Oh, please don't say his name! (*claps his "hands" to his ears*) I get so nervous whenever I hear it.
	Anyway, I've got to find a house, and I spent all my money on candy and allergy medicine. Maybe my friend Artie can help me; I thought I heard his voice up here.
	(*calls to side of stage*) Artie! Are you here somewhere? Artie!
ARTIE:	(*enters*) Did somebody call? Oh, hi, Aaron! How's it going?

AARON: Hello, Artie. I'm in big trouble and I need your help. I have to find a house to live in so that You-Know-Who doesn't get me.

ARTIE: Oh, you mean the Big Bad . . .

AARON: *(claps his "hands" over Artie's mouth)* Don't say his name! I get so n-nervous.

ARTIE: All right, I won't say anything about the Big Bad . . .

AARON: *(shaking)* **Don't say his name!**

ARTIE: OK, OK, calm down. Let me see if I could help you. *(thinks)* Where could you get a house for free? I know! Try my magic word, wizzlewuzzlewoozle. Maybe it'll work for you.

AARON: *(considering it)* I don't know. *(to audience)* Do you think I should try it? *(whether they say "Yes" or "No," he goes on)* All right, Artie. I can't think of anything better.

ARTIE: Just say, "Wizzlewuzzlewoozle . . . "

AARON: Wizzlewuzzlewoozle.

ARTIE: Then you wish for whatever you want and count to three. Have you got it?

AARON: I think so. I hope so.

ARTIE: Good. Hope it works! Good luck! *(they shake hands)*

AARON: Thank you. See you later, Artie.

ARTIE: Bye! *(exits)*

AARON: If there is a later. Well, let's try it out. *(to audience)* Will you help me? Let's say it together. Wizzlewuzzlewoozle, I wish I had a house. One-two-three.

> *(lights flash, noise is heard—Aaron is totally unprepared;*
>
> *runs to the edge of the playboard and hangs on for dear life;*
>
> *finally, a house that looks like an upside-down straw wastebasket appears)*

What's this? *(walks over and peeks through the window cut in one side)* It looks like an upside-down wastebasket . . . but it's got a microwave and a compact disc player! *(ducks under and goes inside; face shows through the window)*

This is great! I'm going to make myself comfortable, but would you let me know if You-Know-Who shows up? Thank you.

Now, let's see . . .

> *(as Aaron looks around inside, the Wolf's head slowly rises over the playboard;*

audience says, "The Wolf! The Wolf!")

What? Did you see him? Where?

(Aaron turns to look, but the Wolf's head has vanished;

this happens twice more;

on the third time, Aaron turns just as the Wolf slowly rises and they face each other, nose-to-nose)

Oh-oh . . . **Ohhh!** *(Aaron jumps back and because he's "wearing" it, the house jumps back with him)* It's him! It's You-Know-Who! It's the **Wolf!**

WOLF: *(speaking slowly, deeply, and in an oily fashion, like an evil game-show host)* Well, well, well. Will you look at this! A little pig living in a wastebasket!

AARON: This isn't a wastebasket, Mr. Wolf. This is my new house!

WOLF: *(laughs evilly)* Well, it won't be your new house much longer. Little pig, little pig, let me come in.

AARON: No! Not by the hair of my chinny-chin-chin!

WOLF: Then I'll huff *(laughs)*, and I'll puff, and I'll blow your house in!

AARON: No! Please don't!

WOLF: Here I go! *(takes three enormously deep breaths)*

AARON: Oh-oh . . .

(Wolf blows house down;

house and Aaron vanish for a second;

then Aaron reappears, dizzy and shaken;

Wolf watches as if he has all the time in the world)

What happened? *(sees Wolf)* Oh, dear.

(to Wolf) Are you going to eat me? *(Wolf slowly nods)* I was afraid of that. Before you eat me, may I ask you a question?

WOLF: *(supremely confident)* Certainly. What?

AARON: Why are your shoes untied?

WOLF: *(as if hit from right field)* What? Are my shoes untied? *(bends over to look, and as he does, Aaron runs offstage; Wolf talks to audience)*

No, they're all tied, and . . . *(turns back to speak to Aaron and suddenly realizes he's gone)* Hey! Where did that sneaky pig go! **RRRAHHH!!**

(runs after Aaron;

there follows a silly chase:

Aaron runs across the playboard panting and puffing and disappears;

then Wolf enters, howling, and runs off;

two run first in one direction, then the other;

Aaron stops to catch his breath)

Where did he go? I'll get him! *(runs off)*

AARON: *(enters)* I'm leaving! I'm going back home to hide in my mom's basement! Goodbye! *(runs off)*

WOLF: *(out of breath and angry)* Where is he? Where is that pig? Nuts! He got away! But I know he has two brothers. I'll get them for sure! *(chuckles and exits)*

BERNIE: *(enters, singing loudly)* Ohh, la la la la **laa,** doodle-dee doodle-dee **doo** . . . (THE SECOND Hel-lo there, everybody! I'm Bernie, the second little pig. I guess you saw LITTLE PIG) what happened when my brother Aaron tried to build a house with the magic word—ha-ha! That old Wolf almost got him. Aaron's been hiding in Mom's basement for the past three days, and he won't come out. We have to slip his food under the basement door, and that means all he can eat is pancakes—ha-ha!

Well, I'm smarter than Aaron, and lots smarter than that old Wolf. I know I can use that magic word to build a **GOOD** house, but first I have to find Artie.

(calls) Artie! Artie! Are you around anyplace?

ARTIE: *(enters)* Did someone call? Oh, hi, Bernie, how's your brother?

BERNIE: Oh, still hiding in the basement. But, hey, I need your magic word to build a **GOOD** house.

ARTIE: Umm . . . I'm not so sure that's a good idea. It didn't work too well for your brother.

BERNIE: Oh, him. He doesn't know which of his feet to use to stand on his head, but I'm lots smarter than him. So what's the magic word?

ARTIE: *(to audience)* Do you think I should tell him?

(to Bernie) Oh, well, all right, but don't say I didn't warn you. It's wizzlewuzzlewoozle, then you make a wish and count to three. Have you got it?

BERNIE: Sure. **No** problem. Thanks a lot. See you later. *(shakes Artie's hand with such force that Artie wobbles offstage)*

ARTIE: Gooood luuuck. Phew! *(to audience)* I think he'll need it. *(exits)*

BERNIE: *(to audience)* Oh-**kay!** Let's do it! Say it with me: wizzlewuzzlewoozle! Here's the smart part—I wish for a house made of wood! That should be tough to blow down. One-two-three.

> *(lights flash, noise is heard;*
>
> *and a house that looks like a pig-sized orange crate with a window in it appears)*

What kind of a house is this? It looks like an orange crate.

(ducks down and enters) Hey, look at this! It's got cable TV! Wow! And a basement with a **POOL TABLE!** I've got to go practice my 8-ball shot. But if you see the Wolf, will you let me know? OK.

> *(Bernie vanishes below;*
>
> *after about three seconds the Wolf's head appears over the playboard;*
>
> *audience shouts;*
>
> *Bernie comes back)*

Did you see him? Where? *(turns, but the Wolf has vanished)* There's nobody here. See you later.

> *(Bernie descends;*
>
> *Wolf ascends;*
>
> *Audience shouts;*
>
> *Bernie returns, and the scene repeats;*
>
> *finally, Bernie and the Wolf rise at the same moment)*

Oh! Hi there, Wolfie! You can't get me! Ha-ha!

WOLF: *(looks at Bernie, then at the audience, and shakes his head, as if to say, "Who is this fool?"; turns back)* Ahem. Well, well, well. Look at this. A little pig living in an orange crate.

BERNIE: **Very** funny. This is my new house!

WOLF: It won't be for much longer. Little pig, little pig, let me come in.

BERNIE: No! Not by the hair of my chinny-chin-chin!

WOLF: Then I'll huff *(laughs)* and I'll puff, and I'll blow your house in.

BERNIE: Ho-ho! Go ahead and try.

WOLF: Very well.

> *(takes three enormous breaths,*
>
> *blows twice,*

and Bernie and the house fall inside the stage with a tremendous crash)

BERNIE: *(reappears dizzy and shaken)* Ohhh. What happened?

(sees Wolf) Hmmm . . . I think I'm in trouble.

(to Wolf) Are you going to eat me?

(Wolf nods)

I thought so. Well, if you're going to eat me, the least you can do is tie your shoes.

WOLF: *(shakes head)* You can't fool me with that old trick.

BERNIE: Oh. Then I guess you don't want to hear about the big green monster standing behind you.

WOLF: There's no big—*(suspiciously but just a tiny bit frightened)* What big green monster?

BERNIE: Oh, yeah, it's awful. It has one big eye, long green claws, and . . .

WOLF: You're trying to fool me, aren't you *(to audience)* Is there really a big green monster behind me?

(Bernie nods to the audience while Wolf isn't looking)

There is? All right, I'm going to take a look, but **no** funny business, pig!

BERNIE: Take a look! See for yourself! It's awful!

WOLF: All right. *(starts to turn, but turns back quickly and says)* But **no** funny business!

(turns to look, and Bernie immediately runs off)

There's **no big green monster** back here—*(turns back)* Hey! You disgusting pork chop! I'll get you yet! Grrr**RRAHH!**

> *(another chase scene, with slight variations on the first,*
>
> *until Bernie returns, panting, to the playboard)*

BERNIE: Whew! I'm getting out of here! I'm *(puff)* going back to Mom's to hide in the basement with my brother Aaron! Goodbye! *(runs off)*

WOLF: *(enters)* Where-is-that-**pig?** *(pounds head on the playboard)* Nuts! Nuts! Nuts! And double nuts!! Got away again! But I know there's a **third** little pig, and this time he won't get away so easily! *(exits in a huff)*

CALVIN: *(sings offstage)* Who's afraid of the Big Bad Wolf, the Big Bad Wolf, the . . .
(THE THIRD *(enters)* Oh, hi, everybody. I'm Calvin, the third little pig. My two brothers
LITTLE PIG) spent all their money on silly stuff, but I saved mine, and I bought a brick

house that's guaranteed wolfproof! It's supposed to be delivered today; I'm waiting for the UPS truck . . .

(*honking offstage*) There it is! Don't go anywhere—I'll be right back. (*exits*)

(*offstage he says*) Thanks a lot. Whew! This thing is heavy! How did they ever get it in the truck?

> (*brick house rises slowly out of the playboard*
>
> *and Calvin appears and sets it up*)

There! My wolfproof brick house! Now I can unpack.

ARTIE: (*enters*) Hey, Calvin! What a great house!

CALVIN: Oh, hi, Artie. Isn't it a wonderful house? It just arrived on the UPS truck, and it's guaranteed wolfproof!

ARTIE: That's great! So I guess you won't need my magic word.

CALVIN: Magic word? No, thanks. I know what happened to my brothers.

ARTIE: Well, I was reading my magic book some more, and I found out what I was doing wrong. You're supposed to count to four.

CALVIN: Four?

ARTIE: Yeah, say wizzlewuzzlewoozle, make your wish, and count to four. Of course I haven't tried it yet.

CALVIN: Well, I'm glad I won't need it.

ARTIE: But don't forget it, just in case. You never know when you might need a magic word.

CALVIN: I won't need the magic word.

ARTIE: Just in case. It's wizzlewuzzlewoozle—and count to four!

CALVIN: See you later, Artie!

ARTIE: Well, goodbye. Good luck! (*exits*)

CALVIN: Why would I need a magic word in my wolfproof house? Oh well, I'd better get busy. I'm going inside to put my dishes away. If you see the Wolf, will you let me know? (*enters house and leans out window*) See you later.

(*Calvin leaves window; we hear sounds of him moving inside house*) Now where should my gravy boat go?

> (*Wolf appears again*
>
> *and the audience shouts;*
>
> *Calvin reappears*)

Is he there? Did you see the Wolf?

(*looks, but nobody's there*) I don't see anybody. Oh well.

> (*Calvin disappears;*)
>
> *Wolf reappears;*
>
> *audience shouts*)

Is he there? (*looks out window*) I don't see him. Could he be behind the house?

> (*Calvin leaves house, walks around looking;*)
>
> *Wolf appears by Calvin's side when Calvin looks away;*
>
> *and Wolf vanishes when Calvin looks toward him;*
>
> *as Calvin is turned away, Wolf rises and opens his mouth to show his teeth;*
>
> *when Calvin turns around again, he's staring down the Wolf's throat*)

Hey, what's this? I didn't know here was a cave so close to my house.

(*feels a tooth*) And what's this? Is it a stalagmite or a stalactite, or . . . wait a minute . . . it's the Wolf!

(*Calvin runs inside and looks out the window at the Wolf*) That was a close one! What do you want, Wolf?

WOLF: Well, well, well. What a cozy little house you have, pig. Such a shame I'll have to blow it down.

CALVIN: You won't be able to blow **this** house down. It's **guaranteed wolfproof!**

WOLF: (*dripping sarcasm*) **Oh, my!** "Guaranteed Wolfproof!" Oh, dear! (*angry now*) We shall see, Mr. Pig. Little pig, little pig, let me come in.

CALVIN: No! Not by the hair of my chinny-chin-chin!

WOLF: Then I'll huff (*laughs*), and I'll puff, and I'll blow your house in.

CALVIN: Go ahead and blow, but you won't be able to blow **this** house in.

WOLF: We shall see.

> (*takes three enormous breaths, and blows against the house three times;*)
>
> *each time, Calvin has a response*)

CALVIN: (*first blow*) That'll make great air conditioning this summer.

(*second blow*) Mr. Wolf, has anyone ever told you you should brush your teeth more often?

(*third blow*) Well, I can't wait around here all day. I've got dishes to put away. See you later, Mr. Wolf. (*leaves window*)

WOLF: (*out of breath*) GrrrRRR!! PIG! GET UP HERE!

CALVIN: (*back at window*) May I help you?

WOLF: You may think you're so smart in your "wolfproof house." But you're going to have to **leave** that house sometime. When you do, I'll be waiting for you . . . right here! And I can wait a long, long time. (*makes himself comfortable at far end of playboard*)

CALVIN: (*to audience*) Oh-oh. I never thought of that. How did he know I don't have any groceries in the house? If I can't leave, I'll starve. What am I going to do?

(*paces back and forth behind window*) I could throw Limburger cheese at him . . . but I don't have any. Do you have any ideas?

(*someone in the audience will suggest the magic word*)

You mean Artie's magic word? That never works . . . but I've got to try something. All right, I'll use it . . . but I can't remember it. Was it fizzlefuzzle or something? (*audience shouts correct word*)

Oh, thanks. Let's try it. Are you ready? Wizzlewuzzlewoozle. I wish, um, I wish the Wolf would . . . I know! I wish the Wolf would turn into a little mouse!

WOLF: Ha! That'll never happen!

CALVIN: Now I'm supposed to count to . . . three? Four? Four! One, two, three, four!

WOLF: (*pause for about three seconds*) There! You see? I told you I would never . . . turn . . . (*begins shaking*) Heeey! Whaaaat's haaapennninng?

(*vanishes; lights, sound, and suddenly a little mouse appears, speaking in a high voice*) Ohhh. I feel . . . funny. Hey—how come you're so big all of a sudden?

CALVIN: It worked! That's because you're a mouse.

WOLF: (*appears as mouse*) I am not a mouse!

CALVIN: (*walking over to him*) Yes you are.

WOLF: Am not!

CALVIN: (*to audience*) Isn't he a mouse? (*audience responds*)

WOLF: I am?

CALVIN: That's right.

WOLF: Oh. Then change me back!

CALVIN: No, I won't change you back, but do you know what I'm going to do?

WOLF: What?

CALVIN: I think I'm going to get myself . . . a cat.

WOLF: (*in terror*) A **cat?** A **cat?** Then I'd better, um, get going. Ah, um, well, see you later. (*looks frantically for a place to run, finds one, and shoots off*) **Goodbye!**

CALVIN: (*watching*) There he goes. I think he's in the next county already. And here comes Artie. Hey, Artie! C'mon over here!

ARTIE: (*enters*) Hi, Calvin. What was that mouse running from? I thought he'd been shot from a cannon.

CALVIN: Oh, that was the Wolf. I used your magic word to change him into a mouse.

ARTIE: You mean—my magic word **worked?**

CALVIN: That's right.

ARTIE: It **worked?**

CALVIN: That's what I said.

ARTIE: It **worked?** It actually **worked?**

CALVIN: For the third time, yes.

ARTIE: Oh, thank you. Mm-mm-mmm-mm! (*kisses Calvin*)

CALVIN: Yuck! What are you doing?

ARTIE: That magic word never worked before! Maybe now **I** can get it to work!

CALVIN: Well, good luck. When you're through, come on in for . . . well, for a glass of water. See you later, everyone! (*exits into house*)

ARTIE: All right! Now . . . for the first time . . . I will do a magic trick correctly. Wouldn't a mighty oak tree look good in Calvin's yard? Here we go. Say it with me: Wizzlewuzzlewoozle. I wish that a mighty oak tree would appear right here in Calvin's yard. One, two, three, four!

(*lights, noise, and a tiny daisy appears*) Oh. I guess some people just aren't meant to be magicians.

(*bends over and smells flower*) And flowers smell nicer than oak trees, anyway. That's the end of the show. See you later, everyone! (*exits into house; curtain*) ■

Production Notes

This script is a very simple one, intended for a one-person performance, although the magic tricks and puppet changes require that both hands be constantly occupied. (See chapter 5 for a description of how the stage is set up for quick changes.) The writing is in the rhythm of everyday conversation. However, the plot develops rhythmically, with the same general sequence of events occurring with the appearance of each of the pigs. The only lines from the original story are those beginning with "Little pig, little pig, let me come in," yet as much of the spirit of the story as possible has been retained.

When I created this show, I made four puppets from scratch (the wolf and the three pigs), and I didn't want to spend much time making scenery, too. So I used things that came to hand—and it worked fine. The First Pig's house was an old woven flowerpot basket (see figure A.1) in which I cut a window about 4" × 4" and sealed the edges with hot glue so they wouldn't fray. The First Pig actually wore the basket over his head—which made both easy for the wolf to "blow" away. The Second Pig's house was a cardboard box about 8" × 8" × 6" in which I cut a window as well. The Second Pig wore his house, too. This may sound weird, but try it; it works (as long as the tops of your pig puppets' heads are fairly flat).

The Third Pig's house was more challenging. I cut a house shape of Masonite, about 10" high and 8" wide, mounted it on a long block of wood, with a dowel set in it that could be placed in a hole near the playboard. The pig can come and go in and out easily, yet when the wolf is onstage, the pig looks through his window and the kids accept that the wolf can't follow him.

■ **FIGURE A.1** Houses for "The Three Little Pigs"

BASKET
FOR FIRST
PIG'S
STRAW HOUSE

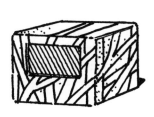

PAINTED
CARDBOARD
BOX FOR SECOND
PIG'S
STICK HOUSE

PAINTED
MASONITE
HOUSE FOR
THIRD PIG'S
BRICK HOUSE

The objects that Artie conjures up are found objects—a coathanger, an artificial flower, or in fact any old thing that you think might surprise and please the audience.

The Three Billy Goats Gruff

Freely adapted from the folktale from
Asbjørnsen and Moe

Characters:

ARTIE, the master of ceremonies, eager to please

TROLL, grumpy and thoroughly nasty

LITTLE BILLY GOAT GRUFF, innocent (but not *that* innocent)

MIDDLE BILLY GOAT GRUFF, smooth and witty

BIG BILLY GOAT GRUFF, a little cowardly but good as gold

Prop:

bridge

SCENE: A bridge over a rushing river

ARTIE: *(enters briskly and stands at one side of the bridge)* Hey! Hi, everybody. Let me introduce myself. *(bows deeply to each side)* My name is Artie, and I'm the master of ceremonies for this puppet show.

Now can anybody tell me what this thing is? *(points to bridge; some child will eventually say "A bridge!")* **Ab**-solutely correct! A bridge.

Now, who can tell me what famous story takes place on a bridge? *(audience responds)* Right! The story of the Three Billy Goats Gruff! And here's how it begins. . . .

Long ago in Norway, over a rushing river, there was a brightly painted bridge. And under the bridge, there lived . . . who? *(audience says, "A troll!")* That's right! It was a mean, nasty, ugly, stinky, smelly old Troll. If he didn't like your looks, he would bite you . . . and if he **did** like your looks . . . he'd eat you.

Are any of you afraid of trolls? *(audience usually says "No!")* Well, I don't know if **you** are, but I sure am, and here he comes now. See you later!

(exits in a hurry, and after a second we hear a gruff voice offstage)

TROLL: *(as he enters)* Ruuuhhff! Raaahh! Hmmm! I smell somebody out there. I definitely smell somebody out there.

	(*sees the audience*) Ahhh! A whole lot of somebodies! Hel-**lo**, heh, heh. You know who I am, don't you? (*"The Troll!"*) That's right, I'm the mean, nasty, ugly, stinky, smelly old Troll, and don't you forget it, either.
	Right now I'm waiting here for my lunch, and do you know what my favorite lunch is? Nice, fresh goat chops. Not pork chops, not lamb chops, but nice, fresh, goat chops—and there's a goat coming right now. Watch me get him, heh, heh, hah. (*slowly descends*)
LITTLE BILLY GOAT:	(*enters*) Tra, la, la—oh, hello everybody. I'm the Little Billy Goat Gruff, and I want to cross this bridge to get over to the other side so I can eat some of the nice green grass. But first I've got to get past (*points downward with his nose*) old Mr. Stinkums down there.
	I've got a plan. I'll say "Courage! Chin up! Shoulders back!" Here I go.
	(*starts across bridge*) Trip-trap, trip-trap—(*stops*) You don't see that Troll anywhere, do you? No? (*starts again*) Trip-trap, trip-trap—(*stops again*) You still don't see him, do you? No? Good. (*starts again; goes one step*) Trip—
TROLL:	(*rears out of the playboard*) **Rrahh!** Hel-lo! Who might you be, tripping and trapping over my bridge?
LITTLE BILLY GOAT:	**Ooh!** Hello, Mr. Troll. I'm the Little Billy Goat Gruff and I want to go over to the other side to get some grass.
TROLL:	Ahhh. Well, here I am to gobble you up.
LITTLE BILLY GOAT:	Please don't eat me, Mr. Troll.
TROLL:	Well, why shouldn't I?
LITTLE BILLY GOAT:	Because you should wait for my bigger brother, the Middle Billy Goat Gruff. He's much bigger, much juicier, and much tastier, too.
TROLL:	(*thinking about it*) Hmm. You're **not** very big . . .
	(*to audience*) What do you think? Should I wait for the bigger one?
	(*while he faces the audience, the Little Billy Goat nods to them frantically*)
	(*faces Little Billy Goat*) Well, all right. Go on, beat it; I'll wait for the bigger one. (*descends*)
LITTLE BILLY GOAT:	(*watching Troll leave*) Goodbye, Mr. Troll. Thank you.
	(*faces audience*) Whew! That was easier than I thought. See you later, everybody! (*crosses the bridge*) Trip-trap, trip-trap, trip-trap, bye! (*exits; after about two seconds, we hear the smooth singing voice of the Middle Billy Goat Gruff*)

MIDDLE BILLY GOAT:	(*enters*) Ohhh, she was on-ly the goat of my dreammms . . .
	(*sees the audience*) Hi there, everyone. I'm the Middle Billy Goat Gruff, and I'd like to get across this bridge as well. I've got a plan of my own. Last night I was reading a scary, scary story and I thought to myself: Maybe, just maybe, if I can make a **really scary** face, I can scare the nose off that Troll. I want to try my scary face out on you first. Are you ready? (*"Yeah"*) You're not going to get too scared, are you? (*"No"*) Okay, here goes.
	(*descends, pauses a beat, then returns*) You're **sure** you're not going to get too scared? (*"No"*) Okay.
	(*descends*) One . . . two . . . three . . . (*jumps up, face slightly askew, making a silly noise*) blubbablubbablubba! (*sees audience is not scared; face returns to normal*) You don't look very scared. All right, I'll make an even **scarier** face. Here goes.
	(*descends*) One . . . two . . . three . . . (*jumps up, jaws askew*) booga-booga-boo! (*sees audience is not scared; face returns to normal*) Oh. You're harder to scare than I thought. This calls for my scariest face of all—my Stephen King special. I've been practicing it in the bathroom mirror. Here goes.
	(*descends*) One . . . two . . . three . . . (*jumps up, face ridiculously contorted*) oooh-wah-ooo**oooo**h! (*audience laughs; face returns to normal*)
	Oh, well. I suppose I'd better forget the whole thing and just do what my little brother did. I'll say, "Courage! Chin up! Shoulders back!" Here I go.
	(*starts across bridge*) Trip-trap—(*stops and looks around*) You don't see him anywhere, do you? No? Good. (*starts again*) Trip-trap—(*stops again*) You're sure you don't see him?
	(*while Middle Billy Goat is facing audience, the Troll pops up silently in his path*)
	Then I'll just—(*turns and sees Troll*) Whoaa! Um, hello, Mr. Troll.
TROLL:	Well, who might you be, tripping and trapping over my bridge?
MIDDLE BILLY GOAT:	I'm the Middle Billy Goat Gruff, and I was just going over to get something to eat.
TROLL:	Ohhh. Well, here I am to gobble you up.
MIDDLE BILLY GOAT:	Please don't eat me.
TROLL:	Why shouldn't I?
MIDDLE BILLY GOAT:	Because you should wait for my bigger brother, the Big Billy Goat Gruff. He's much bigger, much juicier, and much tastier, too.
TROLL:	I already fell for that line once. Why should I wait for the big one?

MIDDLE BILLY GOAT:	Because he's **so** big, you'll be able to eat half of him today and put the rest in the freezer for next week.
TROLL:	(*thinking about it*) Hmmm. Maybe I should.
	(*to audience*) What do you think? Should I wait for the big one?
	(*Middle Billy Goat nods eagerly to audience*)
	Oh, all right. Go on, be off with you. Get out of here. (*descends*)
MIDDLE BILLY GOAT:	Thank you! (*to audience*) Such a pleasant fellow. I'd better get going. (*starts across bridge*) Trip-trap, trip-trap, bye! (*exits; pauses a second; then we hear his voice offstage*) But wait a minute—wait a minute—where is my big brother, anyway? I'd better get back up there.
	(*reenters*) Big Billy Goat! Where is he? Big Billy Goat!
	(*Big Billy Goat appears around the side of the stage, where Middle Billy Goat can't see him;*
	audience says "There he is!")
	Where? (*looks; Big Billy Goat is gone*) He's not there.
	(*Big Billy Goat appears at top of stage;*
	audience says "He's up there!")
	Up there?
	(*Big Billy Goat is gone*)
	You must be the same people who are always seeing flying saucers and Bigfoot.
	(*Big Billy Goat reappears at side of stage*)
	You see him again? I think I know what's going on. This is family stuff, and I don't really like to talk about it, but . . . my big brother is a little bit of a coward. I think the only way we're going to get him up here is to call him up, but you have to yell **really** loud. I'm going to count to three, and then I want you to yell just as loud as you can, "Big Billy Goat!" Ok? Really rip your lungs out, now. One . . . two . . . three . . . **Big Billy Goat!**
BIG BILLY GOAT:	(*enters*) Hey, what's all this noise? You people are giving me a headache!
MIDDLE BILLY GOAT:	You're supposed to come across this bridge!
BIG BILLY GOAT:	Oh, um, I've got a sore throat. I'll do it tomorrow. (*starts to leave,*)
MIDDLE BILLY GOAT:	(*calls him back*) Wait a minute! Get up here. What are you, a goat or a chicken?

BIG BILLY GOAT:	(makes a noise like a hen) Buck, buck, buck, bu-gack.
MIDDLE BILLY GOAT:	Oh, brother. Get over here.
BIG BILLY GOAT:	(to audience) Do you think I should cross? ("Yes") Oh, all right, I'll do it.
MIDDLE BILLY GOAT:	Good. Now just do what we did. Say, "Courage!"
BIG BILLY GOAT:	(obviously unsure about the whole thing) Courage.
MIDDLE BILLY GOAT:	Chin up!
BIG BILLY GOAT:	Chin up.
MIDDLE BILLY GOAT:	Shoulders back!
BIG BILLY GOAT:	Shoulders back.
MIDDLE BILLY GOAT:	All right. Now go get him—**go** for it! And I'll see you later. (exits)
BIG BILLY GOAT:	That's easy for him to say. He's already across the bridge. Well, I said I'd do it, so I'd better do it. Here goes. (hesitates at the entrance to bridge) I'm going. Here I go. I'm going to go. It's time to go. I'd better go. **All right**, I'm going.
	(very tentatively starts) Trip-trap, trip—You don't see him anywhere, do you? No? Maybe he got tired of waiting and left. Maybe he went out and got a cheeseburger.
	(Troll appears for a second where Big Billy Goat can't see, then withdraws)
	Did you see him? Oh-oh. He's not here. Don't make me nervous.
	(Troll plays hide-and-seek for a minute with the Big Billy Goat, then very decisively appears at his side)
	But I don't—**ohh!** Hey, Mr. Troll, that's not nice. You (gulp) better not try any funny business . . . or you'll be . . . sorry!
TROLL:	(mock-contrite) Oh, I'm sorry. I'd better be **very** careful.
	(to audience) I heard this guy making chicken noises. I'm not scared of him.
	(to Big Billy Goat) I'm **so** scared of you, do you know what I'm going to do?
BIG BILLY GOAT:	What?
TROLL:	This. (bites Big Billy Goat on the end of his nose, accompanied by honking sound)
BIG BILLY GOAT:	**Ouch!** You bit me on the nose! That hurt!
TROLL:	Awww. (dripping sarcasm) Did I hurt you?

BIG BILLY GOAT:	Yes.
TROLL:	Awww. I'd better call your mommy so she can put a Band-Aid on it.
BIG BILLY GOAT:	*(to audience)* He's making fun of me. He's making me **mad.**
TROLL:	Oh, boy. If you're so mad, come on and hit me. Come on.
BIG BILLY GOAT:	*(to audience)* Do you think I should hit him? *("Yeah!")*
	(Troll himself nods)
	I usually don't like to hit anybody, but this Troll's nothing but a big bad bully.
TROLL:	Come on, hit me. Nyaah, nyaah, nyaah.
	(Big Billy Goat winds up for a punch;
	Troll chuckles to the audience) Now watch this!
	(there follows a mismatched fight in which the Big Billy Goat winds up and strikes at the Troll several times;
	Troll always leaps out of the way just in time;
	Big Billy Goat's force carries him across the stage uselessly;
	Troll razzes until Big Billy Goat stops, out of breath;
	Troll laughs to the audience)
	Ha ha, what a wimpy goat! He'll never hit me in a million—*(Big Billy Goat knocks Troll over)* **Aaaa**aaaah!!
	(Troll flies off, and a tremendous crash is heard backstage)
BIG BILLY GOAT:	There. I think that took—*(looks down, where the Troll should be)* Oh-oh! Here he comes again. I'd better get ready.
TROLL:	Ohhh . . . *(reenters, dizzy and shaken)* what happened?
	(shakes his head to clear it; is REALLY mad) **All right, goat.** No more Mr. Nice Guy! Here I come! One . . . two . . . three . . .
	(charges; Big Billy Goat is ready and knocks him off the stage again) **Aaa**aaah!!
	(crash)
BIG BILLY GOAT:	That probably—*(sees Troll coming again)* Oh, no. He's coming back a third time. I guess he doesn't know when to give up.
TROLL:	*(moans in background)* Oooohh. Ohhh. *(enters, very dizzy)* Wheerrre's thaaat goaat? I'lllll . . . *(spins around until he falls off the bridge by himself)* Aaaah!!
	(crash)
	(Big Billy Goat watches calmly)

Alllll riiiight, herrre I come. *(appears again, leans on bridge for support)* I'll get you, goat. I'll get you. Just let me . . . catch my . . . breath . . .

(Big Billy Goat calmly picks Troll up by the nose and heaves him lightly over the side) Hey, what, I, leggo, my, **nose! Aaa**aah!!

(crash; three seconds of silence)

BIG BILLY GOAT: *(now feeling pretty good)* Some people just don't know when to quit. Whew! After that I'm so hungry I think I could eat a rock. But now I don't have to . . . I can go get some nice green grass! See you later, everybody! Trip-trap, trip-trap, bye! *(exits)*

TROLL: *(offstage)* Ohhhhh . . . I feel awful . . . *(reappears, completely out of breath)* I feel like all three of those guys took a walk over my face. *(turns upside down by rotating head over)* I feel like every bone in my body is upside down. *(turns back over)*

Do you know what I'm gonna do now? I'm going back to my cave and have a nice glass of warm milk. And I **don't** mean goat's milk, either! Goodbye! Ohhhh . . . *(slips slowly off the playboard and lands backstage with a crash)*

ARTIE: *(as he enters)* . . . and the Three Billy Goats Gruff ate lots of grass, got nice and fat, and the Troll never bothered them again. Thanks a lot for watching our show, everyone. Goodbye! ■

Production Notes

This version of "The Three Billy Goats Gruff" takes about fifteen minutes to perform. Notice, by the way, how I've changed the characters of the goats from the traditional story to suit the children in the audience. I've made the Big Billy Goat the most childlike of the three to make him the easiest for children to identify with, and they do. The Big Billy Goat literally doesn't know his own potential, and the Troll serves as the challenge that forces him to test his abilities.

Scenery and Props   The scenery is very simple; it's just one bridge, as shown in figure A.2. Two semicircular cuts are made in a ½" pine or fir board, 6" × 18". The two sections are separated by 4" lengths of ¼" dowel. The bridge is attached to the stage by 3" lengths of ¼" dowel glued into lower section.

Maneuvers   All the action takes place behind this bridge. Each goat enters at my right and travels to the right. The only really tricky part of this performance is the scene in which the Middle Billy Goat exits, then reappears and calls up the Big Billy Goat. (See the photo.) Throughout the play, the

FIGURE A.2 Bridge for "The Three Billy Goats Gruff"

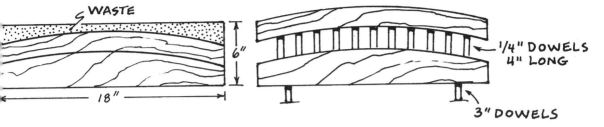

WASTE

6"

18"

1/4" DOWELS
4" LONG

3" DOWELS

goats are always on my right hand and the Troll on my left, but for this scene I take off the Troll (and hold him between my knees) and quickly switch the Middle Billy Goat to my left hand after his first exit. He then reappears on my left side of the bridge, saying, "I wonder where my big brother is." The Big Billy Goat then goes on my right hand for the scene in which he peeks over the side and top of the stage. After the Middle Billy Goat exits, I take that puppet off and put on the Troll while the Big Billy Goat is hesitating at the entrance to the bridge.

Sound Effects   The crashes are made by striking a cocoa tin full of odd metal parts on the floor backstage. Mine is mounted on a rather elaborate foot pedal with springs, but you could also hang it on a string from your prop shelf and kick it if your sense of balance is good.

Who's the Squonk?

Original play by Walter Minkel

Characters:

CYRIL THE CROCODILE, a real show-off

KHAKI THE ELEPHANT, the kind of son every mother would want if she were an elephant

Scenery and Props:

pair of palm trees	stake
vine	*Cat in the Hat* book

SCENE: Along the banks of the Zambezi River in the middle of the summer; palm trees on either side of the playboard

CYRIL: *(entering, wearing sunglasses)* Hey, hey, hey! Cyril Crocodile at your service. What a **bee-you**-tee-full summer day! Just the kind of day to **laze** *(stretches out)* and catch some rays. Watch me get a tan and turn a nice dark green. I'll just . . . hey! What's that?

(Khaki sings, "Hum de dum . . . ," offstage)

Oh, no. It's Khaki the Elephant—yuk, phooey—King of the Ding-dongs! President of the Nerds! Squire of the Squonks!

KHAKI: *(offstage)* Hum de dum de dum. *(enters)* Here's a lovely spot. Hello, Cyril. Isn't it a lovely day?

CYRIL: It was 'til **you** get here. Yuk! Now the whole riverbank will be infested with cooties.

KHAKI: Tsk, tsk. How juvenile. Well, I'll just get my book and make myself . . .

CYRIL: A **book?** Did you say get a **book?**

KHAKI: That's right.

CYRIL: Ha! You read **books** during the summer, when you don't have to? What a squonk!

KHAKI: I beg your pardon. What did you say?

CYRIL: I said, what a squonk! (*gives loud Bronx cheer*)

KHAKI: I am not a squonk.

CYRIL: Yes you are! (*Bronx cheer*)

KHAKI: I am not.

CYRIL: Are too! (*Bronx cheer*)

(*here follows a sequence of "Am not!"; "Are too"; Bronx cheer; until Cyril finally says*) Wait a minute! OK, Bozo, if you're **not** a squonk, prove it!

KHAKI: Very well; **how** do I prove it?

CYRIL: Hey, HEY! (*to audience*) I'm going to have some fun with Khaki—watch this!

(*to Khaki*) Let's see . . . how about a contest? I'll bet I can roar louder than you.

KHAKI: Louder than an **elephant?** Never!

CYRIL: We'll see. You stand over there—(*points to one end of playboard*) and I'll stand here. (*points to other end*) You roar first.

KHAKI: All right. Ahem . . . one, two, three . . . (*trumpets loudly*)

CYRIL: Pretty good—but listen to this!

(*whispers loudly to audience*) Ok, gang, when I count to three I want you to **roar** as loud as you can. All right?

(*to Khaki*) Here we go . . . one, two, three . . . (*huge roar*) there! Now who's the squonk?

KHAKI: That was loud, but . . .

(*to audience*) Was he cheating?

(*to Cyril*) Something funny was going on. I want another contest.

CYRIL: All right, my little squonk. If you want to get creamed again . . . how about a tug of war?

KHAKI: All right. I **know** I can pull harder than you.

CYRIL: Let me find a vine. I'll be right back. (*looks around, exits*)

KHAKI: (*to audience*) I'll show **him** I'm not a squonk. Nobody can pull like an elephant.

CYRIL: (*offstage*) Here we are.

(*enters carrying a vine*) Take this end, (*Khaki does*) and I'll take the other end.

(*to audience*) Now watch this!

(*to Khaki*) Hey, look up there! It's a UFO!

KHAKI: (*looking up, away from Cyril*) Where? What? I don't see anything.

CYRIL: (*while Khaki looks the other way, Cyril shoves a stake into the playboard with his end of the vine tied to it, then hides the stake from Khaki—but not the audience—with his body*) Oh. I guess I must have been seeing things. Are you ready to pull?

KHAKI: All right! Watch this! Let's have the kids count us down. 5–4–3–2–1–**go!**

(*Khaki pulls very hard, grunting and straining;*

Cyril simply holds on to his end of the vine and looks very relaxed)

CYRIL: What's the matter, little squonk? Didn't you eat your Wheaties this morning?

(*Khaki, angry, pulls harder and harder*

until he falls, exhausted, on the playboard;

Cyril, with a flourish, pulls him all the way over;

then Cyril quickly disposes of the vine and stake)

There. Now who's the squonk?

KHAKI: (*out of breath*) I **know** something funny was going on that time. I **demand** another contest.

CYRIL: Well, if you want to get really walloped. . . . How about . . .

KHAKI: No you don't. This time I want to pick the contest.

CYRIL: Well, sure.

(*to audience*) He's so tired out, I'm sure I can beat him in anything.

KHAKI: (*sets his book down on the playboard between them*) Here we are. Whoever can read this page the fastest wins.

CYRIL: Hey, wait a minute! What kind of squonky contest is this? I won't . . .

KHAKI: What's the matter? I thought you could do everything better. You aren't afraid of being the **squonk**, are you?

CYRIL: Who, me? Um, never! Let's do it!

KHAKI: All right. You read first.

CYRIL: Um, okay. Let's see. *(examines the page hesitantly)* Um. "The sun . . . did not . . . shim . . . shine. It was too, um, wet to plan, ah, play. So we sit, I mean we sat in the horse, I mean **house**. . . ." What kind of squonky book is this? Phooey!

KHAKI: *(reads)* "The sun did not shine. It was too wet to play. So we sat in the house all that cold, cold, wet day." It's from *The Cat in the Hat*. **Now** who's the squonk?

CYRIL: Well, um, I guess I am this time.

KHAKI: Don't feel too bad. It took real brains to beat me in those other contests—enough brains to enjoy a good book.

CYRIL: Yeah, you're right. Let's call a truce. No more squonks, ok? Let's be friends.

KHAKI: Friends. *(Cyril shakes Khaki's trunk with his jaws)*

CYRIL: One more thing.

KHAKI: What's that?

CYRIL: Would you read that book to me? That story sounded like it might be pretty good.

KHAKI: Sure! Let's go sit under that palm tree over there. *(exits)*

CYRIL: *(to audience)* Hey, hey! We've got to go, but remember this: How can you tell if an elephant has checked out a library book? When you open it, peanut shells fall out! See you later, alligators! *(dances off)* ■

Production Notes

This play should be quite simple for one person to perform, and even simpler for two. It was written for the Oregon Statewide Summer Reading Program's manual the year the theme was "Summer Reading Safari" and was performed by various library staff people around the state.

Puppets   I made two mouth puppets of an elephant and crocodile with the elephant being a bit larger than the crocodile. I found an elephant puppet pattern and made all the cloth pieces about half an inch too big all over and used lots of stuffing. Then I sewed a pair of mirrored sunglasses on the

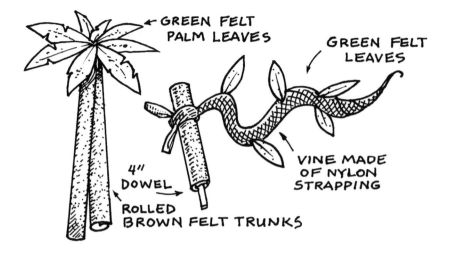

■ **FIGURE A.3** Scenery and Props for "Who's the Squonk?"

crocodile puppet. (Cyril almost always got a laugh just entering with those "cool" sunglasses.)

Scenery and Props   The only scenery was two pairs of felt palm trees about 16" high made of large pieces of felt with pipecleaner ties to attach them to each side of the proscenium (or you could use Velcro). (See figure A.3.)

The stake was a 4" segment of ½" dowel with a ¼" segment of ¼" dowel drilled into the bottom, and a 2' piece of nylon strapping with felt leaves makes the vine. (See figure A.3.)

A copy of *The Cat in the Hat* (which shouldn't be too difficult to find) is the only other prop. I used a "discarded for condition" copy.

Coyote and the Galloping Rock

Adapted from a Sioux tale

Characters:

GRANDFATHER TORTOISE, stuck up, grumpy, and boastful

RABBIT, a walk-on; happy-go-lucky

BIRD, another walk-on; a wise guy

COYOTE, supremely self-confident

IKTOME THE SPIDER, Coyote's sidekick; eager, enjoys Coyote's tricks, but is sometimes irritated by his ego

THE ROCK, ponderous, powerful like a force of nature

Scenery and Props:

    2 blankets   coyote-skin rug

SCENE: Somewhere out on the Great Plains

ARTIE: *(as master of ceremonies)* Hi, everyone! Have you ever heard of Coyote? He's famous among many Native American people for his tricks. Here's one story about Coyote's tricks that comes from the Sioux people, and it takes place out on the Great Plains, right on the edge of the mountains. Can you imagine it? The wind's blowing, sometimes hard like this *(puppeteer makes blowy noise and Artie leans far to one side, hanging on to the stage)* and sometimes not *(blowy noise becomes a little hiss and he stands up straight)*, sometimes cold *(shivers)*, and sometimes very hot *(leans forward, wipes brow)*. Phew! Coyote's on his way here, but first let's meet Grandfather Tortoise. I'll see you later. *(exits)*

GRANDFATHER TORTOISE: *(offstage)* I'm coming! I'm almost there! Here I come! *(enters, with blanket around neck)* Good afternoon, children. I am Grandfather Tortoise, oldest—and wisest—of all the animals. I wanted to show everyone my new and very beautiful blanket. *(shows it off)* Do you see? Isn't it lovely? I just received it from my favorite nephew in Arizona, and I know that nobody around here has a blanket that's quite so fine, that's anywhere near as lovely, that's . . .

RABBIT: *(offstage)* Ha, ha!

GRANDFATHER TORTOISE: *(looks around)* Who's that?

RABBIT: *(pops up and down unseen by Grandfather Tortoise)* Ha, ha!

GRANDFATHER TORTOISE: Who's laughing at me?

RABBIT: *(pops up and stays)* I am!

GRANDFATHER TORTOISE: Rabbit! Why are you laughing at me?

RABBIT: Because I know what's going to happen . . .

GRANDFATHER TORTOISE: What?

RABBIT: Coyote's going to trick you out of that nice new blanket.

GRANDFATHER TORTOISE: He will not!

RABBIT: Yes he will.

GRANDFATHER TORTOISE: Will not!

RABBIT:	You'll see. Good luck, Grandfather Tortoise. *(vanishes, then pops back up)* Ha, ha! *(vanishes)*
GRANDFATHER TORTOISE:	Who does that Rabbit think he is? I'm too smart to be fooled by that Coyote. If he even tries fooling me, he'll find out that I'm a lot smarter than he thinks!
BIRD:	*(appears to the side of, or on the top of, the stage, as if perched on a rock or plant, then disappears)* Ha, ha!
GRANDFATHER TORTOISE:	*(looks around)* Who's that?
BIRD:	*(pops up and down unseen by Grandfather Tortoise)* Ha, ha!
GRANDFATHER TORTOISE:	Who's laughing at me?
BIRD:	*(pops up and stays)* I am!
GRANDFATHER TORTOISE:	Bird! Why are you laughing at me?
BIRD:	Because I know what's going to happen . . .
GRANDFATHER TORTOISE:	What?
BIRD:	Coyote's going to trick you out of that nice new blanket.
GRANDFATHER TORTOISE:	He will not!
BIRD:	Yes he will.
GRANDFATHER TORTOISE:	Will not!
BIRD:	You may think you're smart, Grandfather Tortoise, but you're not as smart as Coyote! *(vanishes, then pops back up)* Ha, ha! *(vanishes)*
GRANDFATHER TORTOISE:	Ooooh! I will not be laughed at like that! Just let Coyote come here! Let him try to trick me! He'll never be able to trick me out of my blanket! Where is he? Where's that Coyote?
	(Coyote appears next to him, but Grandfather Tortoise angrily carries on) I'm older and I'm smarter! Let him try! Let him—
	(notices Coyote) Ah-ha! Coyote! There you are! Well, go ahead.
COYOTE:	What do you mean, Grandfather Tortoise? Go ahead and what?
GRANDFATHER TORTOISE:	I know you're here to trick me out of my blanket. Go ahead and try!
COYOTE:	But I'm not here to trick you out of your blanket, Grandfather Tortoise. I only wanted to see it.

GRANDFATHER TORTOISE:	You can't fool me, Coyote! Go ahead and try to trick me!
COYOTE:	But I can't trick anyone today, Grandfather Tortoise.
GRANDFATHER TORTOISE:	You can't? Why not?
COYOTE:	Because I didn't bring my cheating medicine along. I have to be warm to play a trick. It's not warm enough today without using my cheating medicine, so I'm afraid I can't trick anyone. Sorry.
GRANDFATHER TORTOISE:	*(surprised)* You mean you can't trick me because you're not warm enough?
COYOTE:	That's right. Well, goodbye. *(starts to exit)*
GRANDFATHER TORTOISE:	Wait, Coyote. Now I'm disappointed. I wanted to show you that you couldn't trick me.
COYOTE:	But I can't unless I'm warm.
GRANDFATHER TORTOISE:	*(thinking)* Well, then, um, ah! Here, Coyote. If I cover you with my blanket, will you be warm enough?
COYOTE:	Maybe, if I really concentrate.
GRANDFATHER TORTOISE:	Well, then, let's try. *(removes blanket and drapes it over Coyote's head)* Are you warm enough now?
COYOTE:	No. I'm going to concentrate. Here we go. Hmmmmmmmmmmmmmm. *(weaves back and forth)*
GRANDFATHER TORTOISE:	Well?
COYOTE:	Almost. This isn't as good as my cheating medicine. I need to do it again. Hmmmmmmmmmmmmmm. *(weaves)*
GRANDFATHER TORTOISE:	Are you warm enough now?
COYOTE:	Almost perfect. Watch. HmmmmmmMmmmmMmmm. *(as he weaves, Grandfather Tortoise's head weaves with him)* There.
GRANDFATHER TORTOISE:	All right. Are you ready to trick me?
COYOTE:	I think so. I was going to ask you . . . Grandfather Tortoise! Look! Is that a tornado?
GRANDFATHER TORTOISE:	*(turns away)* What? Where?
COYOTE:	Oh, I guess not. Bye! *(runs off, carrying the blanket)*

GRANDFATHER TORTOISE:	(turns around) What? Hey! Coyote, come back with my blanket!
	(turns to audience) I can't believe it. He tricked me—and I asked him to! Maybe I can get my nephew in Arizona to send me a new blanket.
	(starts to exit, then turns back) I'll get you, Coyote! (exits)
	(pause that signifies a change of location)
COYOTE:	(offstage) Ha! I fooled that Grandfather Tortoise! (enters) You know what his problem is? He thinks I'm going to follow the rules. But rules are for other people, not for me. I want to show this great blanket to my friend Iktome the Spider.
	(calls out) Ik-**to**-me! Where is he? Ik-**to**-me!
	(Iktome peeks out over the top or side of the stage)
	Ik-**to**-me! (sees him) There you are!
IKTOME:	Hello, Coyote. Ah, what a nice blanket! Where did you get it?
COYOTE:	I tricked Grandfather Tortoise out of it. It seems I forgot my **cheating** medicine.
IKTOME:	(comes down to the playboard) You fooled him with **that** old trick?
COYOTE:	What can I say? It worked. And I look rather handsome in this blanket, don't you think? (twirls) Are you feeling hungry, Iktome?
IKTOME:	Yes I am.
COYOTE:	Come on with me, then. I know where there are some chickens we can trick out of their eggs. Come on! Follow me! (exits)
IKTOME:	(to audience) Do you know what I like about being Coyote's friend? He always knows where the food is. Wait for me, Coyote! (runs off)
	(pause)
THE ROCK:	(enters slowly from the other side of the playboard and makes its way across, humming deeply) Ahhh-ummmm. Ahhh-ummmm. (reaches a spot near the other end of the playboard, stops, and is silent)
	(Coyote and Iktome enter from other end)
COYOTE:	We go right down this trail, and . . . (sees The Rock) Ah! Iktome, look at this rock. I've been down this trail a hundred times and I've never seen this rock before. How do you think it got here?
IKTOME:	I don't know, Coyote, but look at it. This rock is very special. It has power. Look at the moss on it—and its strange shape.
COYOTE:	Yes, it is a very handsome rock, isn't it? (considers) Hmmm . . . Do you know what I think I'm going to do, Iktome?

IKTOME: What, Coyote?

COYOTE: The sun's coming out, and it's getting warmer. I think I'm going to give my nice new blanket to this special rock.

IKTOME: You're feeling very generous today, Coyote. But if you give it to the rock, you know you can't take it back. You know what everyone says: "What is given is given."

COYOTE: Ha! Rules are for other people, not for me. Come on, Iktome. Help me put the blanket on this very special rock.

(Iktome climbs atop The Rock and he and Coyote drape the blanket over it)

There! And if I ever want it again, I'll just come and take it back. Come on, Iktome, let's go get those eggs!

(Coyote and Iktome exit)

THE ROCK: *(after a pause, moves slowly in the other direction, humming deeply)* Ahhh-ummmm. Ahhh-ummmm. *(exits)*

(after a pause Coyote and Iktome return)

COYOTE: *(enters, lies down as if he's too stuffed to move)* Ah, what a feast! I've never eaten so many eggs in my life!

IKTOME: That was very, very good, Coyote. And the way you fooled those chickens into . . . Coyote, look!

COYOTE: *(lifts head)* Look at what?

IKTOME: Ooh. There's a big storm coming. *(runs to the end of the playboard)* And the wind is starting to blow!

(puppeteer makes blowing noise;

Iktome is blown back into Coyote)

COYOTE: Oof! And it is getting cold. Do you know what, Iktome?

IKTOME: What, Coyote?

COYOTE: I think I want my blanket back. Be a good spider and go back to that rock and get my blanket back. I'm going to take a nap in my hole. *(starts to descend, but Iktome stops him)*

IKTOME: But Coyote, you know that what is given is given.

COYOTE: Ha! Rules are for other people, not for me. Just bring me the blanket. Good night. *(descends; starts snoring)*

IKTOME: That's what I don't like about being Coyote's friend. I have to do the work he doesn't want to do. *(exits)*

(*pause*)

THE ROCK: (*enters, humming deeply*) Ahhh-ummmm. Ahhh-ummmm. (*stops at end of playboard*)

IKTOME: (*enters from the other end, looking around*) Now where is that rock? There it is. I'd better ask its permission first.

Oh, Rock, I am Iktome the Spider. I ask your permission to take your blanket back.

(*to audience*) Of course, we all know that rocks can't talk.

THE ROCK: **No.**

IKTOME: (*jumps*) "No?" Rock, did you say "no"? (*cowers away*)

THE ROCK: **Yes.**

IKTOME: Oh, you said "yes"? (*comes toward Rock*)

THE ROCK: **Yes, I said "no."**

(*Iktome jumps away again*)

What is given is given. Now go!

(*Iktome leaps into the air, then runs off*)

(*The Rock exits, humming*) Ahhh-ummmm. Ahhh-ummmm.

(*pause*)

IKTOME: (*offstage*) Coyote! Coyote! (*enters, frantic*) Where is that Coyote? Oh, that's right, he's asleep. I'll have to listen for his snoring.

Is he here? (*cocks head to listen at one end of playboard, but hears nothing*)

Or is he here? (*listens at center of playboard, but nothing*)

Maybe he's here.

(*hears loud snoring*) Ah! Coyote! Coyote! Wake up!

COYOTE: (*offstage*) Wha? Huh? (*pops up*) What? Where's my blanket?

IKTOME: The rock wouldn't let me take it.

COYOTE: Huh? What do you mean, the rock wouldn't let you take it?

IKTOME: It said, "No. What is given is given."

COYOTE: Iktome, rocks don't talk.

IKTOME: This one does.

COYOTE: Well then, you go back to that rock and tell it that Coyote wants his blanket back, and if Coyote doesn't get his blanket back, Coyote will be upset. Now go.

IKTOME: All right, but . . .

COYOTE: Go on!

IKTOME: All right. *(exits)*

COYOTE: Hah! Talking rocks! That's ridiculous! I'm going back to sleep. *(stretches and descends out of sight)*

(pause)

THE ROCK: *(returns, humming)* Ahhh-ummmm. Ahhh-ummmm. *(stops at center of playboard)*

IKTOME: *(enters)* Where is that rock. Oh-oh! Look! It's moved! Can this rock walk around, too?

(turns to Rock) Ahem. Rock, this is Iktome the Spider again. I bring you a message from Coyote. Coyote says he wants his blanket back, and if Coyote doesn't get his blanket back, Coyote will be upset. What is your answer?

THE ROCK: **I do not care what Coyote says.**

IKTOME: You don't?

THE ROCK: **No. What is given is given. Now go!**

IKTOME: *(jumps)* Yow! *(runs off)*

THE ROCK: *(exits slowly, humming)* Ahhh-ummmm. Ahhh-ummmm. *(exits)*

(pause)

IKTOME: *(runs back)* Coyote! Coyote! Where is he? Oh, he's still asleep. I'll have to listen for his snoring again.

Is he here? *(cocks head to listen at one end of playboard, but hears nothing)*

Or is he here? *(listens at center of playboard, but nothing)*

Maybe he's here. *(hears loud snoring)* Ah! Coyote! Coyote! Wake up!

COYOTE: *(offstage)* Wha? Huh? *(pops up)* What, Iktome? Where's my blanket?

IKTOME: The rock wouldn't let me take it. It said, "What is given is given."

COYOTE: Did you tell it that Coyote would be **upset?**

IKTOME: Yes.

COYOTE: Well, what did it say?

IKTOME: It said it didn't care.

COYOTE: It didn't **care?** Hmmph! I'll take care of this myself. I have a reputation to keep up! Never send a Spider to do a Coyote's job. Out of my, Iktome. *(stomps off)*

IKTOME: *(starts to follow, then stops)* Oh-oh. I have a feeling Coyote's going to get into trouble. I hope that rock doesn't clobber him. *(exits)*

            (pause)

THE ROCK: *(enters, humming)* Ahhh-ummmm. Ahhh-ummmm. *(stops)*

COYOTE: *(stomps onstage)* Where is that rock? Ahhhh! Hello, Rock! I am the great Coyote, and no one says "No" to me! I'll take my blanket *(yanks blanket off The Rock)*, and I'll show you who is the most clever. *(strikes The Rock with blanket)* There!

            (starts stomping off;

            stops;

            turns to audience) Ha! That was easy! *(exits)*

THE ROCK: *(with a deep sepulchral hum)* Mmmmmm**mmmm! Coyote has insulted me! He must learn that what is given is given, and I shall teach him the lesson!**

            (exits humming) Ahhh-ummmm. Ahhh-ummmm.

            (pause)

COYOTE: *(enters wearing blanket)* Ha! I showed that rock! Iktome! Where'd you go?

            (Iktome peeks around side of stage)

            Iktome! *(sees him)* There you are. Why are you hiding?

IKTOME: I thought that rock was going to clobber you.

COYOTE: No, that rock didn't do a thing, and as you see, I've got the blanket. I don't think we'll hear any more from that rock.

THE ROCK: *(offstage)* Ahhh-ummmm. Ahhh-ummmm.

COYOTE: *(looking around)* What was that? Do you see anything?

IKTOME: *(looks around)* No, Coyote.

THE ROCK: *(offstage)* Ahhh-ummmm. Ahhh-ummmm.

COYOTE: Where's that coming from? Iktome, go up on the cliff and see if you see anything.

THE ROCK: *(offstage)* Ahhh-ummmm. Ahhh-ummmm.

IKTOME:	All right, Coyote. *(exits, then reappears at top of the stage; looks to one side)*
	I don't see anything coming this way.
THE ROCK:	*(offstage)* Ahhh-ummmm. Ahhh-ummmm.
COYOTE:	Good.
IKTOME:	*(looking behind)* And I don't see anything back here.
THE ROCK:	*(offstage)* Ahhh-ummmm. Ahhh-ummmm.
COYOTE:	Good.
IKTOME:	*(at other side of stage)* And I don't . . . **oh no!**
COYOTE:	What is it?
IKTOME:	The rock is coming this way! And it's galloping! Let's go! *(exits)*
COYOTE:	Ha! You run if you want, Iktome. I'm not afraid of a rock.
	(to audience) Who ever heard of a galloping rock, anyway?
THE ROCK:	*(appears at Coyote's side)* Ahhh-ummmm.
COYOTE:	Hello, Rock. What do **you** want?
THE ROCK:	**Coyote, what is given is given. Give me back my blanket.**
COYOTE:	Too bad. It's my blanket again. I make up my **own** rules.
THE ROCK:	**If you do not return my blanket, you will learn a lesson.**
COYOTE:	Uh-huh. And you're going to teach me?
	(The Rock advances toward Coyote with an "Ahhh-ummmm" each time; each time Coyote steps back)
	Don't get any closer.
THE ROCK:	Ahhh-ummmm.
COYOTE:	I said don't get any closer.
THE ROCK:	Ahhh-ummmm.
COYOTE:	If you get any closer, do you know what I'm going to do?
THE ROCK:	Ahhh-ummmm.
COYOTE:	I'm going to run away! Ha ha! *(runs off and leads The Rock on a merry chase,*
	up and down,
	back and forth,
	taunting The Rock, while The Rock stolidly chases him)

THE ROCK: *(humming)* Ahhh-ummmm.

COYOTE: *(stops, out of breath)* Ha! I've lost that silly rock. I think I showed it that you don't mess with Coyote!

(as Coyote speaks, the blanket is hanging on the playboard)

THE ROCK: *(appears and lands on a corner of the blanket)* Ahhh-ummmm.

COYOTE: Hey! Get off my blanket.

THE ROCK: **The time has come, Coyote. Will you give me my blanket or will you learn your lesson?**

COYOTE: I'll never give it back!

THE ROCK: **Very well. One . . . two . . . three!**

> *(they tangle in a fight;*
>
> *Coyote howls and disappears below the playboard;*
>
> *we see The Rock "pounding" Coyote)*

COYOTE: *(offstage)* Hey! What! Ow! Yow!

> *(both disappear;*
>
> *silence for two beats;*
>
> *The Rock starts humming again;*
>
> *it reappears wearing the blanket)*

THE ROCK: Ahhh-ummmm. Ahhh-ummmm. **I think Coyote has finally learned that what is given is given. Goodbye.** *(exits humming)* Ahhh-ummmm. Ahhh-ummmm.

(silence for two more beats)

COYOTE: *(offstage)* Ohhhh. Ow! I feel terrible, and I look worse. Do you want to see what that ridiculous rock did to me? *(audience says "Yes")* All right, but you won't like it. Here I come. One . . . two . . . three.

(on "three," a flat Coyote-skin rug appears hanging over the playboard; wiggles slightly as it speaks) Do you see what that rock did to the great Coyote? Now what am I going to do? I'll have to blow myself up again, but I'll need your help. I'm going to count to three, and when I do, I'll need you to blow as hard as you can. Ready? One . . . two . . . three.

> *(audience blows,*
>
> *Coyote jiggles,*
>
> *then stops)*

No. You didn't blow hard enough. Let's try again, but blow harder, all right? One . . . two . . . three.

> (audience blows harder;
>
> Coyote jiggles harder)

Almost, but you've gotta blow really hard! The Moms and Dads [and/or teachers] have to help, too! Ready? One . . . two . . . **three!**

> (everyone blows;
>
> Coyote jiggles and vanishes)

(pause)

COYOTE: Ohhhh. Oh, my head. (restored to original self, he crawls back onto the playboard,

> tries to stand up,
>
> and falls over)

Ohhh . . . where's Iktome? Iktome! Help!

IKTOME: (enters) Coyote! What happened to you? You look terrible!

COYOTE: And I feel terrible. That rock clobbered me.

IKTOME: Well, I know something that will make you feel better.

COYOTE: Oh, yeah? What?

IKTOME: Grandfather Tortoise just got a new blanket.

COYOTE: (perks up immediately) Really? A new blanket? Thanks, Iktome! I feel better already. I think I'll go pay Grandfather Tortoise a visit. (exits)

IKTOME: I thought that would help Coyote. Let's go see what happens. (exits)

GRANDFATHER TORTOISE: (offstage) Hello, everyone. Grandfather Tortoise here. Would you like to see my new blanket? (audience responds "Yes") I thought so. Here I come, here I come.

(enters wearing new blanket) Here it is—my brand new blanket—and nobody —I mean nobody—is going to trick me out of it this time. And I especially mean Coyote!

BIRD: (suddenly appears over Grandfather Tortoise's shoulder) Ha ha!

GRANDFATHER TORTOISE: Who said that? Bird! Why are you laughing at me?

BIRD: I'm laughing at you because I know what's going to happen!

GRANDFATHER TORTOISE: What's going to happen?

BIRD:	Coyote already knows about your new blanket, and he's on his way to trick you out of it.
GRANDFATHER TORTOISE:	Well, he won't be able to do it this time!
BIRD:	Yes he will!
GRANDFATHER TORTOISE:	No he won't!
BIRD:	Will!
GRANDFATHER TORTOISE:	Won't! You'll see!
BIRD:	Ha ha! *(disappears)*
GRANDFATHER TORTOISE:	Nobody's going to laugh at me this time! Just let Coyote try to trick me! Just let him! I'm wise to him this time. I want him to try, just to show him he can't do it. *(Coyote appears at Grandfather Tortoise's side)* Then he'll see! You'll all see! *(realizes Coyote's there)* Ohhh! Coyote! Go ahead.
COYOTE:	Go ahead and what?
GRANDFATHER TORTOISE:	Go ahead and try to trick me. I know that's why you're here.
COYOTE:	But I'm not. I just heard you had a new blanket, and I wanted to see it.
GRANDFATHER TORTOISE:	Yes, and try to trick me out of it. So go ahead!
COYOTE:	But I'm not going to try and trick you.
GRANDFATHER TORTOISE:	I don't believe you.
COYOTE:	Let me prove it to you. How can I prove to you that I'm not here to trick you?
GRANDFATHER TORTOISE:	Let's see . . . that sounds like an interesting challenge . . . *(paces up and down, thinking)* Ah-ha! I've got it! *(to audience)* This will drive Coyote crazy! *(to Coyote)* All right, Coyote, come with me. *(both go down for a moment while Grandfather Tortoise ad libs some dialog—"This will prove you can't fool me again"— then they return; Coyote holds one end of the blanket in his paws, Grandfather Tortoise holds the other end in his mouth and talks as if there's something in his mouth)*

	Now oo hold un end and U'll hold de udther.
COYOTE:	What's that, Grandfather Tortoise? I can't hear you.
GRANDFATHER TORTOISE:	Ah shed oo hold un end and U'll hold de udther.
COYOTE:	What? I can't understand you.
GRANDFATHER TORTOISE:	(*loudly*) Ah **shed**, oo hold **un** end and **U'll** hold de **udther**!
COYOTE:	I'm sorry, Grandfather Tortoise. I just can't understand you when you have that blanket in your mouth.
GRANDFATHER TORTOISE:	(*exasperated, lets the blanket fall; now only Coyote holds it*) **I said you hold one end and I'll hold the other!**
COYOTE:	Ah! Thank you Grandfather—(*tips to one side as if trying to see behind Grandfather Tortoise*) Hey, who's that behind you?
GRANDFATHER TORTOISE:	(*turns*) Huh? Where?
COYOTE:	Goodbye! Hee, hee! (*runs off with blanket*)
GRANDFATHER TORTOISE:	Huh? What? (*realizes what happened, jaw hangs open, and head slowly turns until he's facing the audience*) I can't believe it. I let him trick me! Let it be a warning to all of you! If you see Coyote coming, you'd better run the other way, or . . . well, he'll probably trick you out of your socks! Goodbye, everyone. I think . . . I think I'm going to go hibernate. (*plods off slowly*) ■

Production Notes

This story, which has been outrageously popular with three- to eight-year-old audiences, is made of pieces from several Sioux legends of Coyote that I put into a blender and mixed into a fractured stew. I was more concerned with communicating the idea of Coyote the Trickster to young children than I was with faithfully retelling the stories.

Puppets   You can substitute any two puppets you have for the Rabbit and the Bird.

Coyote is a glove puppet with paws that can manipulate props.

Iktome is a stick puppet made of a Nerf-clone ball about four inches in diameter mounted on a wooden dowel painted black; his legs are made of pipe cleaners and his facial features of felt scraps. (See figure A.4.) Grandfather Tortoise must be a mouth puppet for the final scene to work.

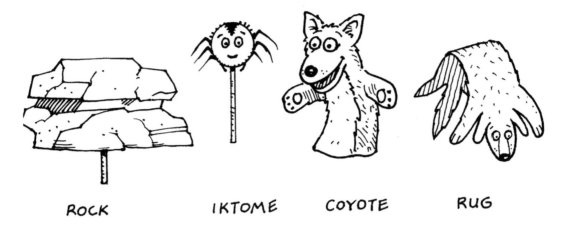

ROCK   IKTOME   COYOTE   RUG

The Rock is another stick puppet made of several glued-together chunks of carved Styrofoam that are mounted on another black dowel. It's flat on the bottom so it can sit on the playboard. The voice of The Rock is as deep, slow, and loud as I can make it.

The coyote-skin rug is simply a flat cut-out Coyote shape of the same fake fur the Coyote puppet was made from. You can hang it over the playboard and jiggle it by the tail.

Props   The blankets are made of felt with a strap to go around the characters' necks and over the top of The Rock (because my sewing skills are so poor).

The Magic Knapsack

adapted from a Danish folktale

Characters:

ARTIE, the fool, not too sharp but definitely likable

ALICE, the good fairy, wants to help—you can tell she majored in social work

THE HOTEL MANAGER, efficient but a bit snobby

EEPY-CREEPS, the evil spirit, rotten but sort of charming as well, as a decent villain should be

Props and Scenery:

knapsack   shawls

hotel desk	fireplace
sausage grinder	sausage
bag of gold	

SCENE 1: In the poor part of town

ARTIE: *(enters, singing with a battered knapsack on back)* Ohhh, I had a little chicken and she wouldn't lay an egg . . .

Oh, hi, everybody. I'm Artie, and boy, do I have a sad story to tell. I used to work in a mattress factory, but I kept falling asleep on the job. Since then I've been wandering around looking for another job, but I haven't found one yet. Now all I have is three cents to my name. I suppose I should be sad, but on a beautiful day like this, I can't.

(sings) Ohhh, I had a little chicken and she wouldn't lay an egg, so . . .

ALICE: *(appears suddenly at Artie's side, wrapped in three old shawls)* Excuse me . . .

ARTIE: *(turns to face her)* Yes? Oh, good afternoon, ma'am.

ALICE: Could you please help a poor woman?

ARTIE: Sure! I mean, I will if I can.

ALICE: Could you spare a penny?

ARTIE: A penny? Well, um . . .

(to audience) Gee, I only have three cents to my name; but I guess there really isn't any difference between three cents and two cents.

(to Alice) Sure, you can have a penny. *(motions as if taking something out of his pocket and handing it to her)* Here.

ALICE: Thank you. Goodbye. *(vanishes)*

ARTIE: Hm! She was in a hurry. Oh well—where was I?

(sings) Ohhh, I had a little chicken and she wouldn't lay an egg, so I . . .

ALICE: *(pops up again, wearing two shawls)* Excuse me . . .

ARTIE: Huh? *(turns and sees her)* Oh, hi. May I help you?

(to audience) She looks awfully familiar.

ALICE: Could you please help a poor woman?

ARTIE: Sure, if I can.

ALICE: Could you spare a penny?

ARTIE: A penny? Well, I guess there's not much difference between two cents and one cent. Here you are.

ALICE: Oh, thank you. Goodbye. (vanishes again)

ARTIE: Hm! She was in a hurry, too. Where was I? Oh, yeah . . .

(sings) Ohhh, I had a little chicken and she wouldn't lay an egg, so I poured hot water . . .

ALICE: (pops up again, wearing one shawl) Excuse me . . .

ARTIE: Huh? What? Oh, hello. Could I help you?

(to audience) I **know** I've seen her before.

ALICE: Could you please help a poor woman?

ARTIE: Wait. Don't tell me. You want a penny.

ALICE: Why, yes! How did you know?

ARTIE: Just a guess.

(to audience) I only have one cent left. But I guess there's not much difference between one cent and no cents, and everyone always tells me I have no sense anyway.

(to Alice) Sure. Here you go. (gives her his last penny)

ALICE: Why, thank you. Goodbye. (vanishes)

ARTIE: Hm! Where have I seen her before? Oh, well.

(sings) Ohhhh, I had a little chicken and she wouldn't lay an egg, so I poured hot water up and down her leg.

(hears a loud noise, like a cross between a whistle and a police siren) Oh-oh. I didn't think my singing was that bad.

ALICE: (rises behind Artie in a long "good fairy" white gown that had been concealed by the shawls) Artie . . .

ARTIE: What? (turns and sees her) Oh! Who are you? You look awfully familiar.

ALICE: I'm Alice, your good fairy, and I'm here to reward you.

ARTIE: Reward me? For what?

ALICE: For your generosity. You gave your last three cents to three poor women. All those poor women were me, of course.

ARTIE: Ok! So that's where I saw you before.

ALICE: In exchange for your three cents, I shall grant you three wishes.

ARTIE: Oh! Thank you. Right now?

ALICE: Right now. Go ahead; what would you like?

ARTIE: Oh, um, let me think. Nobody's ever granted me three wishes before.

ALICE: Come, come Artie; there must be something you'd like.

ARTIE: Oh yeah! But what? Let me think, let me think . . . I know. They always say that health is better than wealth, so I wish to live a hundred years.

ALICE: Very well; your wish is granted.

> (flourishes her arms at him;
>
> a tinkling noise is heard;
>
> Artie wobbles as if something has hit him,
>
> then he stands up straighter)

What's your second wish?

ARTIE: Wooooh! I feel healthier already. Now what? Let me think. I know! I wish for good luck.

ALICE: You shall have it. Your wish is granted.

> (tinkling sound;
>
> flourishes her arms again;
>
> Artie wobbles again)

And your third wish?

ARTIE: Now what? Hmm . . . I could wish for money, but I'd just spend it. I could wish for a car, but I don't know how to drive. . . . I know!

ALICE: Yes?

ARTIE: See my old knapsack here? It's been with me through thick and thin. I wish that whatever I wished to be inside my knapsack would appear inside, and it would stay there until I take it out.

ALICE: An . . . unusual wish. But it shall be granted nevertheless.

> (tinkling sound;
>
> flourishes arms;
>
> Artie wobbles)

Use it wisely. I shall be watching out for you. Good luck, Artie, and goodbye! (whistling siren noise; she vanishes)

ARTIE: Alice, wait! Oh. I didn't even get to thank her.

Hmmm . . . You know, now that she's left, I almost wish I'd wished for some dinner. A nice fried chicken and a salad with French dressing, an ear of nice fresh corn . . . mmm! I wish (*chuckles*) I had **those** things inside my knapsack.

> (*tinkling noise;*
>
> *Artie bows back a little as if something has suddenly fallen into his knapsack*)

What's this? Hey! (*sniffs*) I can smell chicken and French dressing in my knapsack! What I wished for did appear! Let's eat!

Hey . . . I just thought of something. If I can wish for food, maybe I can wish for enough money to stay in a hotel tonight! No more sleeping under a bridge for me. See you at the hotel.

(*sings*) Ohh, I had a little chicken and she wouldn't lay an egg . . . (*exits*)

SCENE 2: The Lobby of the Ritz Hotel

HOTEL MANAGER:	(*bustles onstage carrying the registration desk, which he sets up on the playboard, and begins dusting it off*) Good evening, good evening, and welcome to the Ritz Hotel. I am the manager. It certainly has been busy today. Every one of our rooms is filled. Well, **almost** every one. All of them except for the, ahem, **haunted** room. We never rent that out any more. The last eight people who stayed in that room were (*gulp*) never seen again. I'm glad no one else has come in to ask for a room.
ARTIE:	(*singing as he enters*) Ohh, I had a little chicken . . . Hi, mister. Are you the manager here?
HOTEL MANAGER:	(*a little distastefully*) Yes. May I help you?
ARTIE:	Yeah. I'd like a room for tonight.
HOTEL MANAGER:	(*to audience*) This fellow doesn't look as if he could afford to stay here. (*to Artie*) Our rate is sixty dollars a night.
ARTIE:	Oh, that's Ok. I wish I had sixty dollars in my knapsack. (*tinkling sound*) I've got it. (*turns to show the knapsack*) Take a look for yourself.
HOTEL MANAGER:	Ahem, I believe you. But we don't have any rooms available, anyway. We're all filled up for tonight.
ARTIE:	Now wait a minute. There's something fishy going on. I think you're trying to get rid of me. (*to audience*) Does he have a room? (*audience responds "Yes!"*) (*turns to manager*) Oh, no rooms, hmm?
HOTEL MANAGER:	Well, there is one room, but we don't let anyone stay there any more. It's . . . it's haunted.

ARTIE: Haunted? Aw, come on. There's no such thing as ghosts.

HOTEL
MANAGER: Sir, the last eight people who spent the night in that room have never been
seen again!

ARTIE: Sounds like a story to me. I want to stay in that room tonight.

HOTEL
MANAGER: I don't think that's such a good . . .

ARTIE: In fact, I demand to stay there. Come on!

HOTEL
MANAGER: Very well. But don't say I didn't warn you. This way, please.

(picks up the desk; he and Artie carry it out as they exit) By the way, for this
room I'll need to be paid in advance . . .

SCENE 3: The Haunted Room

*(Hotel Manager and Artie enter, carrying a fireplace; they set it up on the
playboard)*

HOTEL
MANAGER: Well, here you are. I'm sure you'll be quite comfortable . . . for a little
while.

ARTIE: I'll be Ok. I'm not afraid of ghosts. See you in the morning.

HOTEL
MANAGER: Maybe I'll see you . . . and maybe I won't. Goodnight. *(exits)*

ARTIE: Goodnight.

(to audience) Whew! Isn't that a ridiculous story about ghosts? I mean,
everybody knows there's no such thing. Do you guys believe this room is
haunted? *(usually the audience responds, "Yes!")* Oh, come on! Well, I think
I'll take a shower, and then . . .

(horn honk, and Eepy-Creeps's head pokes up behind Artie) What was that?

(turns around, but there's nothing there) Just hearing things, I guess.

(horn honk, Eepy-Creeps's head pops up on top of stage) There it is again. Did
you see anything?

(audience responds "Look up!") Up? Where?

(looks up, but Eepy-Creeps's head is gone again) Somebody's playing a trick
on me! I'm going to go talk to that manager right . . .

(turns to one side, and Eepy-Creeps pops up right before his nose) Oh! Um,
good evening. Who are you?

EEPY-CREEPS: I am Eepy-Creeps, the evil spirit who haunts this room.

ARTIE: Well, pleased to meet you. I'm Artie, and I'm staying in this room tonight. Nice place you've got . . .

EEPY-CREEPS: Perhaps you don't understand. Nobody who stays in this room ever leaves alive!

ARTIE: Aw, that's not a very nice way to treat a guest.

EEPY-CREEPS: Do you know what I'm going to do to you?

ARTIE: No. What?

EEPY-CREEPS: Watch this. I'll be right back.

(exits momentarily;

clanking and rustling down below as Eepy-Creeps sings to himself)

Oh, I'll eat him boiled, I'll eat him fried . . .

(returns with device labeled "Acme Sausage Grinder") Here we are. Do you know what this is?

ARTIE: A sausage grinder?

EEPY-CREEPS: That's right. And do you know what I'm going to do with it?

ARTIE: Make breakfast?

EEPY-CREEPS: (very smarmy now) That's ri-ght! And guess who my breakfast is going to be?

ARTIE: Me? I wouldn't try that if I were you.

EEPY-CREEPS: Why not? Here I come. (slowly begins advancing on Artie)

ARTIE: I'm warning you; you won't like it.

EEPY-CREEPS: Ha! What can a little donut hole like you do to me? (keeps advancing)

ARTIE: All right. I wish you were inside my knapsack.

EEPY-CREEPS: In your knapsack? (laughs) That's the silliest . . . (begins to shake; tinkling sound) Hey! What! **Ohh!!**

(vanishes;

Artie jerks backward suddenly,

and then begins jumping around and wobbling as if something big and powerful was trying to escape from his knapsack)

(angry and muffled) Hey, let me out of here! You can't do this to me!

ARTIE: Sure I can. You aren't a very nice host. Maybe now you'll tell me why you haunt this room.

EEPY-CREEPS:	No!
ARTIE:	Well, I'll leave you in there for a few weeks and . . .
EEPY-CREEPS:	Wait! I'll tell you everything. I was put into this room by an evil magician to guard his bag of gold. It's . . . behind the fireplace. Now let me out of here so I can grind you into a sausage!
ARTIE:	(shakes from side to side as Eepy-Creeps struggles inside the knapsack) I guess you'll never learn. There's just one thing to do, then.
	(shouts) Mr. Manager! Mr. Hotel Manager!
HOTEL MANAGER:	(offstage) Yes?
ARTIE:	I caught your monster for you.
HOTEL MANAGER:	(enters) You . . . what?
ARTIE:	Here he is, in my knapsack. Help me take care of him. Help me get this thing off . . .
	(they struggle with the violently shaking knapsack;
	finally get it off Artie's shoulders;
	Artie holds it over the sausage grinder)
	Do you see the switch on this sausage grinder?
HOTEL MANAGER:	(points) This one here?
ARTIE:	Right. When I give the word, flip it on. Ready? One . . . two . . . three!
	(shakes out the knapsack over the sausage grinder
	just as the Hotel Manager flips the switch;
	they hear all sorts of noise)
EEPY-CREEPS:	(yells) Hey! Ouch! Stop! Ooh! Yow!
	(finally the grinder stops)
HOTEL MANAGER:	What happened?
ARTIE:	Let's open this little door here, and . . . it worked! (both lift up a big sausage with Eepy-Creeps's face) Here's your monster! Changed into a sausage! (sausage is still wriggling and struggling, but the Hotel Manager finally gets it in a firm grip)
EEPY-CREEPS:	Let me go! You can't do this to me!

HOTEL MANAGER:	We already have. Do you know what I'm going to do to you?
EEPY-CREEPS:	What?
HOTEL MANAGER:	You'll make a very nice breakfast, served up in the morning with scrambled eggs. It's off to the freezer with you. (*exits with the Eepy-Creeps sausage*)
EEPY-CREEPS:	(*yells*) Stop! Wait! I'll be good!
ARTIE:	Now let's see . . . first I'll get rid of this sausage grinder . . .

> (*carries it offstage;*
>
> *clunk sound;*
>
> *returns*)

Now let's check behind the fireplace. (*peers inside*) Nothing in there.

(*pushes on it, and it moves a little*) Hey! It's moving!

HOTEL MANAGER:	(*enters*) That takes care of that . . . but what are you doing to the fireplace?
ARTIE:	Give me a hand here; there's a secret panel! (*they push the fireplace a short way*) There! Look!

(*squeezes behind the fireplace and returns with a heavy sack*) Here's the bag of gold the monster was guarding!

HOTEL MANAGER:	Gold? Hidden here all this time?
ARTIE:	That's right. I'll tell you what—since there must be at least a million dollars worth of gold here, why don't we split it three ways?
HOTEL MANAGER:	**Three** ways?
ARTIE:	Yeah. A third to me, a third to you, and a third to help poor people. What do you say?
HOTEL MANAGER:	It sounds good. (*they shake hands*) Now let's go celebrate! The monster's finally gone!

(*they pick up the fireplace and bag and exit*)

SCENE 4: Back on the street again.

ARTIE:	Well, I think my good luck, my long life, and my magic knapsack came in awfully handy. I'm rich, and I can do whatever I want. There's one thing I can't do, though. I wish I could thank Alice for helping me. (*Alice slowly rises up behind him*) But I guess I'll never see her again.
ALICE:	Artie . . .

ARTIE: Huh? *(turns, sees her)* Alice! It **is** you! I'm so glad to see you again. I wanted to say "Thanks" for all you've done for me.

ALICE: But Artie, I only helped you a little. You were the one who was courageous enough to face Eepy-Creeps and trap him in your knapsack.

ARTIE: Well, I couldn't have done it without your three wishes.

ALICE: Thank you, Artie.

ARTIE: *(shyly)* There was one more wish I wanted to make . . .

ALICE: *(teasingly)* Yes?

ARTIE: Well, I wanted to wish . . . that you and I could get married, and I could buy us a trip to Tahiti with my gold.

ALICE: All right. Your wish is granted.

         (to audience) I was hoping he'd wish that.

         (to Artie) But you don't need to spend your gold to fly to Tahiti. All I need to do is wish us there.

ARTIE: Oh. I guess you're right. Then let's go! We'll get married there!

ALICE: Hold my hand. *(waves her other arm)* One . . . two . . . three . . . Here we go! Goodbye, everyone! *(they begin to shake)*

ARTIE: See you later! Whoaaah!

         (crashing sound,

         then a siren sound,

         and finally they vanish;

         stage lights flash,

         then all is silent) ■

Production Notes

"The Knapsack" is a folktale from *Favorite Fairy Tales Told in Denmark,* retold by Virginia Haviland (Little, Brown, 1971). I also read other versions and used the skeleton of the story to create something new. In the Haviland version Artie's character is a soldier home from the wars with only three cents in his pocket, the hotel is an inn with a haunted room and a haughty landlord, the room is haunted by three demons, and in the end the soldier marries his longtime sweetheart. I have tried to keep the spirit of the story, yet simplify and modernize it. Folklore purists will not approve; yet I believe I am being faithful to puppetry as a living oral art form.

Scenery and Props   The props and scenery are simple. (See figure A.5.) None are needed for the first and last scenes, since it doesn't really matter where they take place.

For the second scene, I have a fancy piece of parqueted wood with a little sign reading "Ritz Hotel" and a dowel to fasten it to the playboard to serve as the hotel desk. For the scene in the haunted room, the only scenery piece is a shallow wooden box made into a fireplace and mounted on a single dowel so it can swing to one side.

The most elaborate piece in the show is the sausage grinder. I made it from a big pine block painted red, a piece of plastic pipe, an aluminum pot-pie tin, a light socket and a red 15-watt bulb, and a couple of pipe cleaners. The cord on the light socket leads down to a foot pedal from an IBM dictaphone I found in a junkshop. I wired it so that while the sausage grinder is "on," I step on and off the pedal rapidly so the light flashes. It's really not necessary to be this elaborate; just use your imagination and whatever junk you have at hand.

Other props include two shawls, made from fabric scraps and closed with a little bit of Velcro. A small cloth bag that is filled with buttons represents the bag of gold. The knapsack is a denim or green cloth sack with Velcro straps to cling to Artie's clothes. The sausage is a stuffed cloth tube, one end of which has a little replica of Eepy-Creeps's features cut from felt and glued on.

Maneuvers   As for the actions, there are only two tricky scenes. In the first scene, when Alice keeps appearing, she first appears with three shawls covering her, then two shawls, then just one. As a solo puppeteer, it isn't easy to remove one shawl at a time because Artie's on the other hand, and he's onstage throughout the scene. Well, the answer is a simple one—each time Alice vanishes, I remove one of the shawls with my teeth and let it

■ **FIGURE A.5**   Scenery and Props for "The Magic Knapsack"

drop to the floor. You might want to put Velcro squares on each shawl to keep it in place until it's removed. Just practice doing it, because it's easy to pull more than one shawl off at once (especially using your teeth).

The other tricky bit of business takes place when Eepy-Creeps is transformed into a sausage. The Eepy-sausage is a prop, not an object, but he's supposed to be talking and wriggling. It's up to Artie and the Hotel Manager to struggle with the sausage, almost dropping it at times, to give the illusion that the sausage is alive. As you rehearse this, pretend that the sausage is the proverbial "hot potato" that you can't hold tight, yet can't drop, either.

Sound Effects   Sound effects can be as simple or complex as you wish to make them. A small bell hung from the prop shelf can be nudged with your knee for the tinkling sound. I use a kazoo mounted on a coat hanger around my neck, a triple bulb horn on the floor to step on, and my "crash pedal" (a cocoa can filled with nuts and bolts that I've mounted on a spring-loaded pedal) for dramatic crashes. Singly or in combination, the sounds they make add another dimension to the appearances and transformations. Play around and have fun!

APPENDIX B

STAGE-BUILDING PLANS

Following are plans and directions for two stages for solo puppetry, both of which can easily be converted to two-person stages. Both have survived at least 250 performances and still look almost as good as new. Each can be folded up to fit into a small car with a hatchback. They have been used both indoors and outdoors with audiences of up to 300 children and have produced almost no complaints of "I can't see." Both of these stages are among the lightest, easiest to build and assemble, and most portable full-sized stages around. However, they are neither *very* solid nor *very* stable.

Before you begin building a puppet stage, give some consideration to who is going to use it and how it is going to be used. These stages are intended for one or two adults or teenagers presenting simple hand-puppet shows with fewer than eight total puppets and without elaborate staging. Both require the puppeteers to perform standing up. Neither is suitable for use by more than two people, for use by young children, or for permanent installation in a classroom or library. (Both of these stages should be folded up and stored when not in use.) Their light weight, ease of assembly, and portability mean that they are not able to withstand the rough-and-tumble of children actually using them, nor are they able to support complex scenery pieces or intricate props. For most purposes, however, they are excellent amateur and "semipro" adult puppeteer stages.

Construction of the one-person version of both stages is described in these instructions. The materials lists include those needed to construct both a one-person and a two-person version. Construction should be identical for both sizes with only the width of the stage front adjusted for two puppeteers.

Closed Proscenium Stretched-Cloth Stage

The closed proscenium stretched-cloth stage described here has sides made of cloth that is stretched over a frame of canvas stretcher bars. It is stronger and sturdier than the open proscenium PVC pipe stage described later in this appendix. Additionally, the stretched-cloth stage can use a front curtain. The stretched cloth doesn't wrinkle.

Materials

BASIC FRAME

artist canvas stretcher bars:

    4 at 40" (for a two-person stage, substitute 48" or 50" size)

    8" at 20"

    12 at 36"

    1 piece of wood 38" × 1$\frac{1}{2}$" × $\frac{1}{2}$" for proscenium bar (for a two-person stage, substitute a piece 46" or 48" long)

    4 flathead wood screws 3" long or 4 pieces of $\frac{1}{4}$" dowel each 2" long

    6 screw-in rubber appliance feet (optional)

CLOTH COVERING

6$\frac{1}{2}$ yards of heavyweight cotton/polyester blend fabric at least 45" wide (for two-person stage, use 8$\frac{1}{2}$ yards at least 50" wide or sew 2 pieces together)

HINGES

4 yards of 1$\frac{1}{2}$" cotton or nylon strapping

PROP SHELF

    1 piece of plywood $\frac{1}{4}$" or $\frac{3}{8}$" × 6" deep and as wide as front of stage

    4 small screw eyes

    about 24" of string

    3 small hinges with appropriate number of screws

    rounded wooden molding as long as the shelf length

PLAYBOARD

    1 piece of hardwood 39" × 4" × $\frac{1}{2}$" (for two-person stage, substitute a piece 47" or 49" long)

    2 pieces of hardwood 38" × 1$\frac{1}{2}$" × $\frac{1}{2}$" (for two-person stage, substitute a piece 46" or 48" long)

CURTAINS

    2$\frac{1}{2}$ yards of textured black polyester at least 45" wide (wider for two-person stage)

    2 pieces of $\frac{3}{4}$" dowel, each 42" long (or 50" or 52")

    4 pieces of $\frac{1}{4}$" dowel, each 2$\frac{1}{2}$" long

    2 pieces of Velcro 2" each

RECOMMENDED TOOLS AND SUPPLIES

saw	screwdriver
drill with $\frac{1}{4}$" and $\frac{5}{16}$" bits	staple gun with $\frac{1}{2}$" staples
carpenter's square	craft glue

jigsaw, coping saw, or scroll saw	measuring tape
pencil	chalk
hammer	doweling jig (optional)

DIRECTIONS

1. Find an art supply or paint store that sells canvas stretcher bars, pieces of wood of various lengths that fit together into square or rectangular frameworks onto which you can stretch and staple canvas or cloth. Prices vary widely for these, so shop around.

2. Fit your stretcher bars together into the frame sections 1 through 1.6 shown in figure B.1. It isn't necessary to glue or nail the assembled frames together unless you feel you must; once the cloth is stretched and stapled over them, they hold together amazingly well.

3. After each section is assembled, make absolutely sure that each corner is a 90° angle.

4. Choose the cloth. It should be neither too bright nor too dull. Very bright—red or yellow—cloth will get dirty easily and will "steal the show" from your puppets. Neutral, pleasant-to-the-eye shades of blue, green, violet, or brown are best. Light-colored vertical stripes on a dark background is a good, and not too loud, pattern for a puppet stage. Unless you want to line it, the cloth needs to be

■ **FIGURE B.1** Sections for a Closed Proscenium Stretched-Cloth Stage

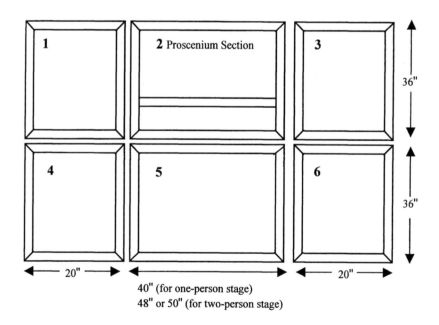

fairly opaque—so your audience cannot see you moving around backstage—and water resistant.

5. Wash and dry the material before assembling it on the stretchers.

6. Lay the cloth right-side down on the floor, and place the section of framework you wish to cover on top of it. Be sure that the grain or pattern of the material runs in the same direction on all sections.

7. With a piece of chalk, trace completely around the frame 3" from the frame.

8. Cut out the cloth for each section, making a diagonal cut at each corner up to about ¼" from the frame so you can fold a square corner.

9. Tack the cloth securely to the wood with a staple gun—a regular stapler will not do the job—stretching the cloth very tightly as you go. To get the cloth to stretch evenly, put about five staples across the first side, then go to the opposite side and shoot five staples. (See figure B.2.) Continue with the two remaining sides. Then go back and staple until you have a staple approximately every 3" on all four sides.

10. Tucking the cloth in at the corners is done like gift-wrapping a package—make sure that none of the wood shows on the edges. (You will, of course, see the wood on the insides of the frames.) Look at prestretched artist canvases in an art supply store if you haven't done this sort of thing before.

11. Follow this procedure for all sections except the proscenium section, section 2. See the following directions for this slightly trickier job.

■ **FIGURE B.2** Section of Stretched-Cloth Stage with Top and Bottom Stretched and Stapled

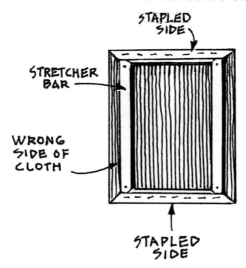

12. As an option, you may want to purchase some screw-in rubber appliance feet to attach to the bottom of sections 4, 5, and 6, using two screw-in feet per section.

THE PROSCENIUM SECTION

You will need to insert a wooden bar in section 2 to serve as the support for your playboard and the lower edge of your proscenium opening.

1. To place the proscenium bar at its proper height, measure the elbow height of the person who will be using the stage. That person should stand comfortably and hold out his or her arm as shown in figure B.3. Measure the distance between one inch above the elbow and the floor. Subtract 36" from that number, and you have the distance between the bottom of section 2 and the top of the proscenium bar.
2. Use 3" flathead wood screws to attach the bar inside the stretcher-bar frame, or if you're a good carpenter, doweling it would be even better.
3. Be sure all angles are right angles, and stretch the cloth over the frame as described previously.
4. Next, cut out the proscenium opening about 2½" inside the frame, making diagonal cuts to the corners of the wood.
5. Staple the cloth around the inside of the opening. (This is a tricky operation, and you will need to check your work frequently from the other side of the frame as you go.)

HINGING

Hinging the three upper and three lower sections together could be the most expensive and difficult part of your job if you were to use metal piano hinges—but by using cloth or nylon strapping, it's one of the easiest and cheapest. When you are finished, the lower half of the stage—sections 4

■ **FIGURE B.3** The Proper Height for the Proscenium Section

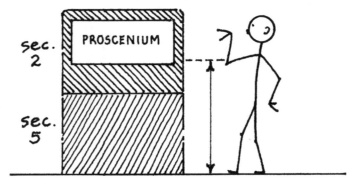

through 6—will be hinged together. The upper half will also be hinged together.

1. Cut the strapping into four 36" lengths.
2. If you use nylon strapping, quickly hold the cut ends over a flame (a gas stove burner works fine, but be careful) until the filaments melt together slightly to prevent fraying.
3. Place the completed wood-and-stretched-cloth sections side by side (sections 1, 2, and 3 in one group; sections 4, 5, and 6 in the other). Their sides should be touching and their top and bottom edges should be aligned exactly.
4. Lay the strapping on the two adjacent sections as shown in figure B.4.
5. Staple the strapping to both sections, using staples about every 3".

DOWELING

The best way to fit the two three-panel segments (the top half and the bottom half) of the stage together is to dowel them.

1. Lay the two segments on the floor together wrong side up. Align them exactly.
2. Mark with chalk points that are 3" from the outside of each of the individual sections. (See figure B.5.)
3. Using a doweling jig if you can get one (if not, you'll need steady hands), drill holes about 2" deep into the top and bottom edges of the sections, through both cloth and wood. A good dowel size is $1/4$", and a good drill bit size for the holes for the bottom edge of sections 1 through 3 is $5/16$". For the holes into which the dowels

■ **FIGURE B.4** Hinge Straps for Sections 4, 5, and 6 of a Stretched-Cloth Stage

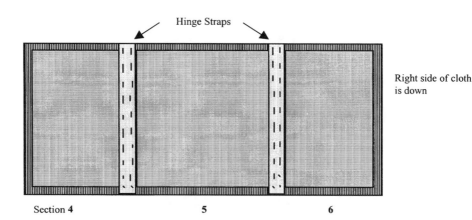

Section 4   5   6

■ **FIGURE B.5** Holes and Dowels to Join the Top and Bottom Halves of a Stretched-Cloth Stage

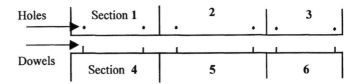

will be glued on the top edge of sections 4 through 6, use a ¼" bit. Then hammer the dowels in.

4. Glue the dowels into the three lower sections, and let them dry. The two sections should fit together properly and be surprisingly stable.

PROP SHELF

You will probably be a happier puppeteer if you add a prop shelf.

1. Use a 6"-deep piece of plywood and hinge it to the bottom back surface of the proscenium section so it can fold up against the section when the stage is folded up.
2. Glue a strip of molding to the outer edge to keep props from rolling onto the floor.
3. Attach screw eyes and string mounted as in figure B.6 to keep the shelf hanging at the proper 90° angle when in use.

PLAYBOARD

The playboard is the actual "stage-floor"—the strip of wood upon which your puppets will perform. You will need three pieces of ½" wood to build it. Use hardwood if possible because the playboard will get lots of use.

■ **FIGURE B.6** Fold-Down Prop Shelf for a Stretched-Cloth Stage

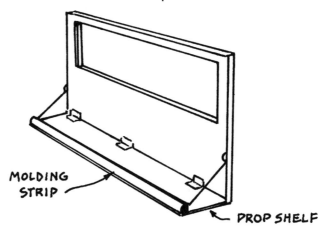

MOLDING
STRIP

PROP SHELF

■ **FIGURE B.7** Playboard for a Stretched-Cloth Stage

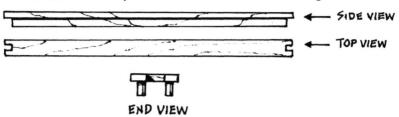

1. Make the square notch cut at each end of the longest board with a jigsaw, coping saw, or scroll saw. The distance between the insides of the two notch cuts should be the same as the length of your proscenium bar for a snug fit. The wood should protrude another inch on the sides of the notch cut. (See figure B.7.) This isn't necessary, but it makes the playboard more stable.
2. Screw or dowel the two thin pieces to the underside of the playboard to hold it in place on the proscenium bar.
3. Either paint or cover the board with several coats of Varathane or a similar protective coating.
4. You may want to include electrical wire staples at regular intervals on the inside edge to attach props and scenery pieces like the Three Pigs' houses and the Three Billy Goats Gruff's bridge.

CURTAINS

With audiences of small children, pausing between scenes, closing front curtains, changing scenery, and then opening the curtains plays havoc with already short attention spans. Therefore, I don't use front curtains and don't recommend them. My puppets change the scenery as part of the show. If you insist on having front curtains, though, Marjorie Batchelder's *Puppet Theatre Handbook* (Harper, 1947) has several good ideas.

Whether or not you use a front curtain, however, you will need a scrim—the curtain that will be an inch or so in front of your face—and a rear curtain behind you. (See Figure B.8.) Both can be made from rough-textured black polyester material through which you (but hopefully not the audience) can see. The scrim allows you to see out without being seen because there is much more light outside the stage than inside.

1. Test your fabrics carefully for transparency.
2. Make the scrim long enough to hang 1" below the level of the playboard.
3. Fasten the bottom of the scrim to the sides of the stage with pieces of Velcro.
4. Make the rear curtain about 5' long. Its purpose is to keep light from behind from silhouetting you and to discourage curious audience

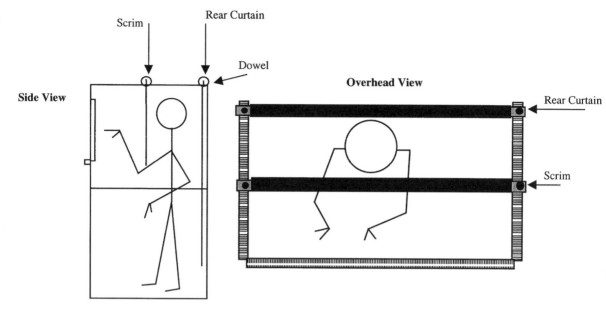

members from coming around the back and watching you instead of the puppets.

5. Hang both curtains from ¾" dowels (the curtain rods) with ⁵⁄₁₆" holes drilled near each end.
6. Glue ¼" dowels about 2" long into the top edges of sections 1 and 3.
7. Fit the curtain rods over these smaller dowels. (See figure B.8.)

Miscellaneous Niceties

ELECTRICITY AND LIGHTS

Several options are available for providing this stage with lights and electricity. However, unless you want to spend a great deal of money, the easiest lights are clip-on lamps with 60-watt bulbs, available for less than $10 in many discount stores. Metal lamps last longer than plastic ones. Clip the lamps to the upper bar of the proscenium opening and keep the cords out of the way by stapling small loops of Velcro along the top and sides of the proscenium opening. You can plug the lamps into a specially made outlet box or a power strip that is hung by hooks and screw eyes from the bottom of your prop shelf or the upper bar of section 5. (See figure B.9 showing the route of the cord and power strip inside the stage.) Plan on having at least 25' of cable or extension cords with you at all times.

■ **FIGURE B.9**   Lighting Configuration for a Stretched-Cloth Stage

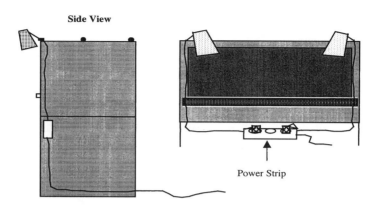

Side View

Power Strip

■ **FIGURE B.10**   Method for Keeping Puppets Ready for Use

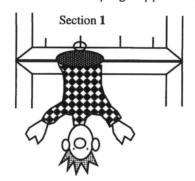

Section 1

PUPPET HOLDERS

You may want to place dowels in the upper surfaces of the bottom stretcher bars of sections 1 and 3 to hang your puppets. Small café curtain rings sewn to the bottom of each puppet allow you to hang them upside down and slip in and out of the puppets easily with one hand. (See figure B.10.)

TOTE BAG

A bag for the stretched-cloth stage can be made out of 4 yards of ripstop nylon and 4 yards of cotton or nylon strapping. Velcro or a zipper can be used to close the bag at the top. Make the bag deep enough to hold both sections of the folded stage stacked together plus the playboard and curtain rods. If you're handy with a sewing machine, you might even make long outside pockets for the playboard, curtains, and perhaps the lights as well.

1. Simply lay the sections of the stage on 4 yards of ripstop nylon.

2. Trace around it with chalk, allowing for thickness and hems.
3. Offset the strapping so you can slip the upper loop onto your shoulder and grab the lower loop comfortably with your hand. (See figure B.11)

■ **FIGURE B.11** Tote Bag for a Stretched-Cloth Stage

Open Proscenium PVC Pipe Stage

The open proscenium stage described here is made almost entirely of PVC pipe. This makes it lighter in weight and slightly cheaper to build than the stretched-cloth stage. In addition, it folds up much smaller than the stretched-cloth stage.

Because this stage has an open proscenium—meaning that there is no proscenium arch over the heads of your puppets—you cannot use a front curtain or attach scenery to the arch, as you might with the stretched-cloth stage. The open proscenium has the advantage, however, of giving more of your audience a clear view of the action without a proscenium arch to block their view. Without a front curtain, you have the puppets change the simple scenery themselves as part of the show.

Materials

BASIC FRAME
a total of 48' of ¾" (or ½") polyvinyl chloride (PVC) pipe:

5 pieces 36" long (for two-person stage, substitute 5 pieces 48" long)

2 pieces 30¼" long	2 pieces 26½" long
2 pieces 20" long	2 pieces 18½" long
2 pieces 17" long	2 pieces 15" long

| 4 pieces 14" long | 6 pieces 9" long |
| 2 pieces 3" long | 10 pieces 2" long |

PVC connectors:

    16 T connectors

| 4 pieces of 90° corners | 2 pieces of 45° corners |

2 pieces of ⅝" wooden dowels (for curtain rods) 2" longer than the stage width

4 rubber cup-type furniture feet 1¼" size

CLOTH COVERING

4 yards cotton/polyester-blend material at least 45" wide

PLAYBOARD

1 piece of hardwood 38½" × 4" × ½" (for two-person stage, substitute a piece 50½" long)

1 piece of hardwood 36" × 4" × ½" (for two-person stage, substitute a piece 48" long)

2 pieces of ¼" dowel, each 4" long

1 yard Velcro

2 yardsticks cut to 20" each

PROP SHELF

1 piece ¼" plywood, 38" × 6" (for two-person stage, 50" long)

2 pieces rounded molding, the length of the plywood

2 pipe clips with accompanying nuts, washers, and bolts

CURTAINS

2½ yards textured black polyester at least 45" wide (wider for two-person stage)

2 pieces of ¾" dowel, each 39" long (or 51" for two-person stage)

4 pieces of ¼" dowel, each 2½" long

RECOMMENDED TOOLS AND SUPPLIES

saw	screwdriver
drill with ¼" and ⁵⁄₁₆" bits	PVC cement
contact cement	measuring tape
pencil	router or dado blade on power saw
2 yards Velcro	

Directions

PVC pipe construction is like playing with adult Tinkertoys. The PVC stage is basically a light, spare frame of pipes with cloth hung over it to conceal the puppeteer and the puppets.

PVC pipe costs as little as 89¢ for a 10' section on sale; its primary use is for lawn sprinkler systems. The connectors cost between 25¢ and 89¢ each.

You can use either ¾" or ½" pipe for the one-person stage; ½" pipe makes for a lighter, but slightly wobblier, stage. For a two-person stage, use ¾" pipe. Because the pipe fits together so securely and is so light, you can pick up the one-person stage and move it around the room without having to disassemble it. For performing outdoors, you will need to stake it down with tent stakes and cord or weight it with sandbags if it is in a windy spot.

1. Cut the pipe into the listed lengths. Figure B.12 shows an exploded diagram of the stage with the segments of pipe and their location.
2. Fit the pipes together. The dimensions of the pipes are, you will discover, not exact; it may be necessary to trim off ⅛" or ¼" in places so the stage will not lean.
3. To make assembly easier, glue the pipe segments and connectors with PVC cement into push-together sections. Use extreme care when gluing. With PVC cement, once you slip a connector filled with glue onto a pipe, you have only 20 seconds or so to make adjustments; lay them down on a level floor and press hard immediately after gluing. Be certain that one T-connector is absolutely parallel with another if there is to be one at each end of a pipe. Figure B.13 shows the glued-together sections, each small enough to fit into a standard duffel bag.

With the exception of the side sections of the performance area, my own stage is divided into many separate sections to make transportation easy. You might want to experiment with different configurations for your stage. I have assembled the stage in about 8 minutes; once you get assembly down, it's quite fast. There are 8 main upright pipes to the stage, and they're often difficult to tell apart. You might want to color code the pipes and the connectors they fit into with permanent ink markers (at the dots marked in figure B.13) so assembly will be quicker and easier.

PROP SHELF

As shown in figure B.14, the prop shelf consists of 4 T connectors, 5 pieces of pipe, a 6" deep section of plywood the width of your stage, strips of molding, and pipe holders. It will be the largest and heaviest portion of the stage.

1. Cut and sand a piece of ¼" plywood 6" deep and as wide as the front of the stage.
2. Glue ½" molding strips to the long sides of the shelf piece. (These are to prevent props from rolling off the shelf.)
3. The supporting frame of PVC is made of 4 T connectors, 2 sections of 2" PVC pipe that connect the T connectors on each side, and

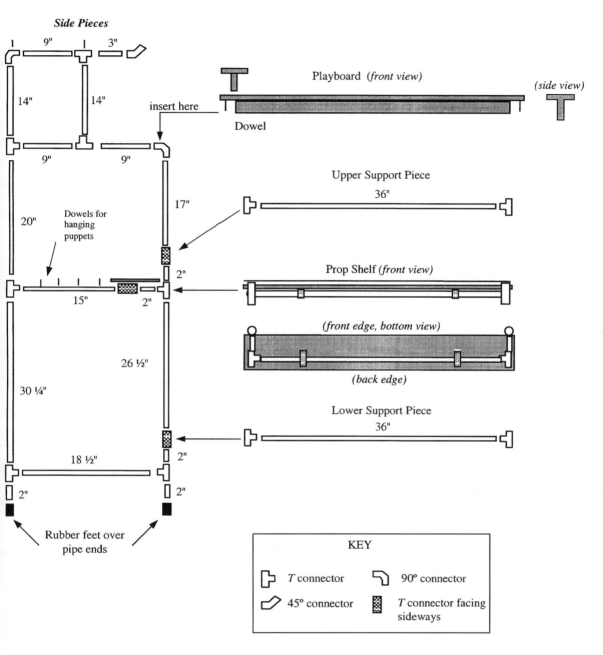

FIGURE B.13 Sections of a Permanently Glued PVC Pipe Stage

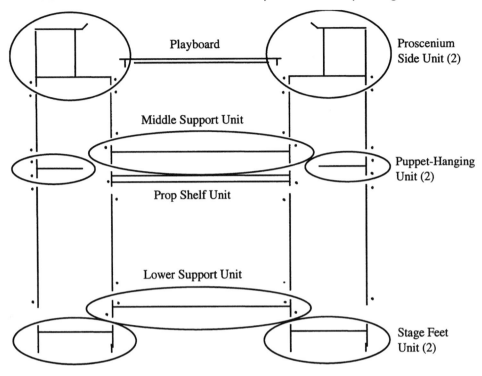

FIGURE B.14 Prop Shelf for a PVC Pipe Stage

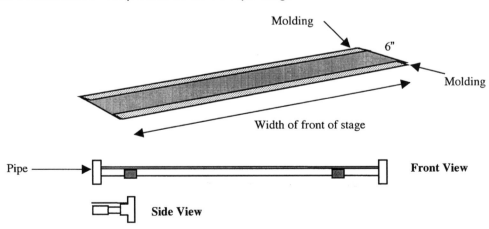

a piece of PVC pipe that's 36" for a one-person stage (or 48" for a two-person stage). Glue these together as shown in figure B.14.

4. Drill holes in the shelf, and attach the PVC frame to the plywood shelf using brass pipe clips.
5. Bolt an electrical power strip to the shelf if you use lights and sound.

PLAYBOARD

1. Cut two pieces of $\frac{1}{2}$" × 4" hardwood to the width of your stage.
2. If you have a router or a dado blade on your power saw, cut a $\frac{1}{4}$" deep dado in the upper portion of the playboard as shown in figure B.15.
3. Glue and clamp the lower portion in place.
4. Staple a yard of Velcro across the lower piece to hold the stage covering in place, as shown in figure B.15.
5. Glue two 4" pieces of $\frac{1}{4}$" dowel in place to be inserted into the 90° PVC connectors at the corner of the large proscenium-side pieces.
6. The proscenium side pieces should have 20" sections of yardstick attached. (It's a shame 18" sections don't work—you'd only have to buy one yardstick.) Glue or staple Velcro to the yardstick sections so you can attach the cloth covering. (See figure B.15.)

CLOTH COVERING

The cloth you use to cover the stage should be very much like the cloth used for the stretched-cloth stage. Unlike the stretched-cloth stage, however, this cloth covering will be removed from the stage each time you disassemble

■ **FIGURE B.15** Playboard Assembly for a PVC Pipe Stage

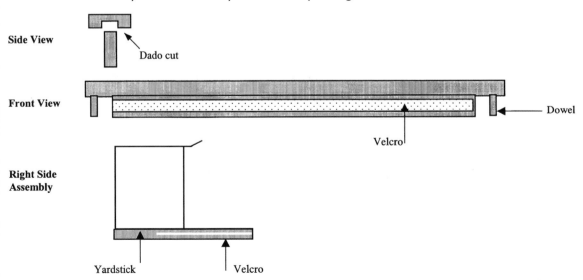

it. See the directions for the stretched-cloth stage for considerations when choosing the cloth and its colors or patterns.

There is no sense wishing you had an exact pattern; the nature of the PVC pipes is such that a cloth covering must be individually fitted to each stage. Go slowly and check that the covering fits on the assembled frame as you go. Figure B.16 shows the approximate layout of the sections of the cloth covering. The thick black line is the location of the Velcro (on the wrong side of the cloth to match the Velcro on the playboard and yardstick sections). Heavily shaded areas indicate where the cloth can be removed to shape the proscenium opening. Small black squares are pieces of Velcro that meet around the upright pipes at the rear of the stage. The drawing on the right of figure B.16 shows how the Velcro on the playboard matches the Velcro on the covering.

1. Wash and dry the material before you sew it so it will do most of its shrinking (if it's going to do any) before you begin working on it.
2. Measure the distance between the bottom of the playboard and the floor. Allow about two extra inches for hemming.
3. Cut the material to cover the front of your stage.
4. Cut the remaining material in half lengthwise.
5. Hem it at the bottom, and sew it to the sides.
6. Temporarily fit it around the stage with safety pins.
7. With chalk, sketch around the area that needs to be removed.
8. Trim it to fit.

■ **FIGURE B.16**   Layout of Cloth and Velcro for a PVC Pipe Stage

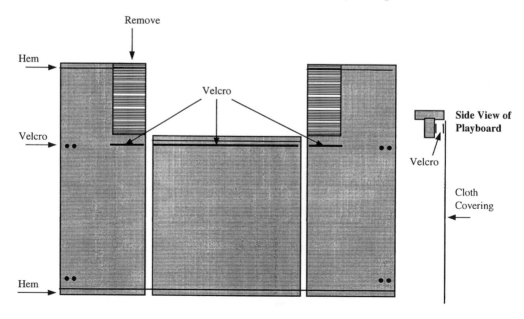

CURTAINS

Like the stretched-cloth stage curtains shown in figure B.8, the PVC stage uses two curtains—a scrim (behind the puppets and in front of the puppeteer's face) and a back curtain (behind the puppeteer and covering the back of the stage). These curtains should be made from a textured black polyester material (to discourage wrinkling) through which you can see.

1. Check the material carefully in the store before you buy it—if it's too opaque, you won't be able to see the puppets; if it's too sheer, the audience will be able to see you.
2. See steps 2 and 4 in the curtain section of the directions for the stretched-cloth stage for measuring the correct curtain lengths.
3. Glue ¼" dowels into the pipes at the top of the proscenium side units.
4. Hang the curtains from ¾" dowels fitted over the ¼" dowels at the proscenium sides.
5. Hem the curtains.

Additional Niceties

ELECTRICITY AND LIGHTS

Lights for this stage are a little trickier than lights for the stretched-cloth stage, but you have several options for mounting your lights. The 45° angle connector at the corner of each of the proscenium side units is intended to hold a light bar. If you're handy with wires, you can buy a clip-on lamp, remove the "clip-on" portion, and glue or bolt the main portion of the lamp into a pipe about 15" long. (See figure B.17.) The cord simply wraps around the pipe, which is painted black.

For more flexibility, you might want to construct a light bar that spans the entire proscenium area. (See figure B.17.) Side bars should be approximately 15" long, but their length will depend on the lights you use. The pipes then are to be inserted in the 45° connectors in the corners of the proscenium side units. Clip the lights (with the help of some well-placed screws or bolts to keep the clips from slipping) onto the bar. Cords loop around the pipes and travel down to a power strip on the prop shelf. Any pipes that are exposed should be painted flat black.

TOTE BAG

The PVC stage will probably fit in a large duffel bag with a zipper. When selecting a duffel bag, take the prop shelf (the biggest single piece of the stage) to the store with you and put it in and take it out, making sure it goes in and out easily.

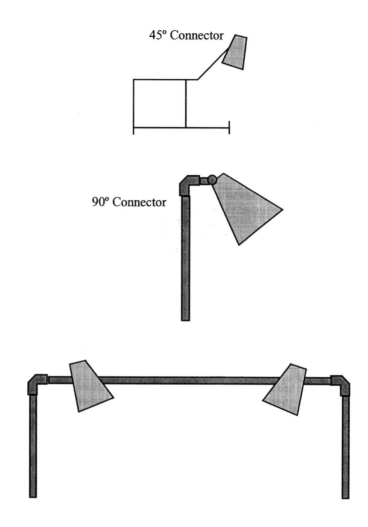

45° Connector

90° Connector

APPENDIX C

SOURCES AND RESOURCES

On the Net

Newsgroup
rec.arts.puppetry

This newsgroup on the Internet allows you to ask questions of those who practice the art of puppetry. It isn't a very busy newsgroup, however. (I get the feeling that most of the puppeteers out there are not spending a whole lot of time on the Net.) Check with your Internet service provider about subscribing.

Puppetry Home Page
http://sagecraft.com/puppetry/index.html

On the Web, one stupendous site is the Puppetry Home Page. Run as a volunteer effort by Rose Sage, it lists and links to most of the best of the puppetry materials and sites available on the Web, including pages with material on puppetry in several cultures worldwide. It also features some beautiful photos of professional puppets to inspire you.

Puppeteers of America
http://www.puppeteers.org/

The most useful resource for anyone in the arts, of course, is other people. If you can, join a regional puppetry guild affiliated with the Puppeteers of America. The people there are enormously helpful. The P of A (as members call it) also produces national and regional puppetry festivals throughout the United States that anyone who is interested in all the possibilities of puppetry should consider attending.

Tales of Wonder
http://darsie.ucdavis.edu/tales/

If you're looking for stories that might be converted to puppetry performances, you might want to visit the *Tales of Wonder* site. It includes brief stories from many cultures that look like good candidates for adaptation.

Books   Anderson, Dee. *Amazingly Easy Puppet Plays: 42 New Scripts for One-Person Puppetry.* Chicago: ALA, 1997.

A good collection of script ideas for the beginning school or library puppeteer. Included are directions for making almost no-sew puppets; a list of suggestions for using puppet "body language" to convey emotions; and appendixes of puppet patterns, scripts, and suppliers.

Champlin, Connie. *Storytelling with Puppets.* 2d ed. Chicago: ALA, 1998.

A nicely done update of the original edition by Connie Champlin and Nancy Renfro. Champlin offers lots of great ideas on how to mix puppets, children, and stories.

Chesse, Bruce. *Puppets from Polyfoam: Spongees.* Portland, Ore.: Puppet Concepts, 1990.

————. *Making and Using Puppets in the Primary Grades.* Portland, Ore.: Puppet Concepts, 1992.

This book and videotape are designed for the beginning puppeteer/educator and are available only through mail order. They show how to build simple but effective mouth puppets from foam rubber—and then what to do with the puppets once they're made. You can order either the book or video or both from Puppet Concepts Publishing, P.O. Box 15203, Portland, OR 97294-5203.

Engler, Larry, and Carol Fijan. *Making Puppets Come Alive: A Method of Learning and Teaching Hand Puppetry.* New York: Taplinger, 1973.

Absolutely the best guide to hand puppet manipulation ever created. It takes puppeteers step-by-step through the process of moving puppets so the audience thinks the puppets are real. I can't recommend it strongly enough.

Hunt, Tamara, and Nancy Renfro. *Celebrate!: Holidays, Puppets, and Creative Drama.* Austin, Tex.: N. Renfro Studios, 1987.

Isn't it funny how parents look for puppet shows—and librarians want to put them on—around holidays and other special occasions? Here's a guide that will give you plenty of ideas.

————. *Puppetry in Early Childhood Education.* Austin, Tex.: N. Renfro Studios, 1982.

A classic, this is the best book I've seen on working with puppets and young children. The book includes lots of ideas for simple puppet making and story interpretation.

Sierra, Judy, and Robert Kaminski. *Multicultural Folktales: Stories to Tell Young Children*. Phoenix, Ariz.: Oryx, 1991.

The book includes stories from around the world, with ideas for sharing them through storytelling and puppetry. It also includes flannel board stories and tips.

Store

John and Jeanine Bartelt, Co-Directors
The Puppetry Store
1525 24th St. SE
Auburn, WA 98002-7837
Phone: (253) 833-8377
Fax: (253) 939-4213

If you want to buy puppetry books for your library or your personal collection, the Puppetry Store of the Puppeteers of America is the place to go. The Puppetry Store carries books, puppet patterns, and other puppetry-related materials you won't find elsewhere. It often keeps out-of-print items in stock far longer than the bookstore jobbers do. For a complete catalog, send $3 to the address above.

INDEX

━━ ▪ ━━

accents, 20
action (on stage), 33, 52–3
adaptation
    advantages of, 27–8
    and copyright, 30–5
    of folktales, 30
    of stories, 32–5
    vs. original, 30
attitude (of performer), 14–16
audience, 33, 68–9
    and accents, dialects, or
        speech irregularities of
        characters, 20
    assistance from, 48
    bonding/communicating
        with, 15
    and improvisation, 50–1
    script writing considerations,
        28–9
audiocassettes (to learn lines),
    52

body language, of puppets,
    20–6
    in character, 21
    eye contact, 21, 22–3
    floor level, 21–2
    hand positioning for glove
        puppets, 23–5
    mouth puppet manipulation
        and voice, 25–6
    movement, 21
bottlers, 72–3
breath control, 17
Bruwelheide, Janis H., 31

chaos, controlling, 73–4
characters
    creating, 16
    staying in character, 21

in story adaptations, 33
voices for, 18–20
children
    behavior of, 69–70, 71–4
    relationship with puppets,
        9–10
classic tales and sensitivity
    issues, 35–40
"climbing stairs" method of
    entrance, 26
closed proscenium stage, 61–2,
    130–40
communication through
    puppets, 8–10, 15
community outreach, 76–8
conflict, 33
copyright, 30–2
    fair use, 31–2
    requesting permission, 32
The Copyright Primer for
    Librarians and Educators, 31
"Coyote and the Galloping
    Rock," 37–8, 104–18
creative control, 41–2

desire (to perform with
    puppets), 2, 13
dialects, 20
dialogue, 33

educational messages in puppet
    shows, 13
entrances and exits, 26
eye contact (puppet), 21, 22–3
eyes (puppet), 57

fair use. See copyright
finger puppets, 10–11
flexibility

program, 48, 76
scheduling, 42
floor level, 21–2
folktales, adapting, 30

gender issues, 39–40
glove puppets, 10
    anatomy of, 24–5
    hand positioning for, 23–5
    and props, 59, 66
"The Gunniwolf," 39–40

hand position
    for glove puppets, 23–5
    for mouth puppets, 23, 25
hand puppets, 10–11
hand-and-rod puppets, 59–60
humor, 33

improvisation, 42, 45–6, 50–1

language, 29, 33
line of death, 71

"The Magic Knapsack," 118–29
manipulation of puppets, 20–6
    eye contact, 22–3
    hand positioning for glove
        puppets, 23–5
    mouth puppets and voice,
        25–6
marionettes. See string puppets
mascots, 42–6
    sample introductory dialogue
        for, 43–5
    silent, 43
memorization, 52

message (of performance), 13, 15

mouth puppets, 10, 58
    hand positioning for, 23
    as hand-and-rod puppets, 59
    manipulation of, 25–6
    as mascots, 43
    and props, 66
    speech movements of, 25–6
movement (of puppets), 20, 21, 57–8

Noe, Marie, 10, 69–70
nonstages, 64

The Old Woman and Her Pig & Ten Other Stories, 32
One Fine Day, 29
open proscenium stage, 62, 140–8
original vs. adaptation, 30
over-the-head stage, 61

performers, traits of, 14–16
phrasing, 17–18
pitch (voice), 18–19
plot, 30
"popping up" method of entrance, 26
problem solving, 50
programs
    activities for, 74–6
    and another puppeteer, 54
    format, 75
    length of 74–5
    in libraries, 69–74
    outside libraries, 76–8
    planning, 51
    solo, 41–54
props, 33, 66–7
    as puppets, 67
    puppets handling, 59, 66
    size of, 50, 67
    storytelling with, 46–7
proscenium, defined, 62
Punch-and-Judy, 36–7
puppetry
    as an art, 1, 12–13
    attraction of, 7

and community outreach, 76–8
    defined, 7–8
    and educational messages, 13
    goals of, 13
    history of, 8, 36–7
    as part of job, 68–78
    performing in a library, 69–73
    working with another puppeteer, 54
puppets, 55–60
    alternative uses of, 75
    children's relationship with, 9–10
    communicating through, 8–10, 15
    eyes of, 57
    handling of props, 59
    kinds of, 10–12
    manipulation of, 20–6
    mascots, 42–6
    movements of, 57–8
    props as, 67
    qualities of, 56–60
    scale/style of, 58
    storytelling with, 46–8

quality (voice), 18–19

relaxation, 17
repetition, 29
rhythm (voice), 18–19
Rockwell, Anne, 32
rod puppets, 12

sample program activities, 74–6
scale (of puppets), 58
scenery, 65–6
    changing, 33, 53
script writing, 28–30
    audience considerations, 28–9
    language and plot, 29–30
    physical considerations, 28
scripts, reading from, 51–2
sensitivity issues, 35–40
    gender, 39–40
    villains, 38–9
    violence, 36–8
shadow puppets, 12

simplicity of programs, 50
solo puppet programs, 41–54
    format, 75
    planning, 51
    suggestions for performing, 49–53
space limitations, 70–1
speech irregularities (of characters), 20
speech movements, 25–6
stages, 60–4
    closed proscenium, 61–2, 130–40
    factors in choosing, 63–4
    nonstages, 64
    open proscenium, 62, 140–8
    over-the-head, 61
stick puppets, 12, 47–8, 58
stories, adapting, 32–5
storytelling with puppets and props, 46–8
string puppets, 11
style (of puppets), 58

technique, 14–26
    attitude, 14–16
    breath control, 17–18
    creating characters, 16
    entrances and exits, 26
    manipulation, 20–6
    voice, 18–20
The Teeny-Tiny Woman, 29
The Three Bears & Fifteen Other Stories, 32
"The Three Billy Goats Gruff," 16, 29, 38, 92–100
"The Three Little Pigs," 29, 80–92
    adaptation of, 34–5

villains, 38–9
violence, 36–8
vocabulary, 33
voice, 17–20
    accents and dialects, 20
    for multiple characters, 18–20
volume (voice), 18–19

"Who's the Squonk?," 100–4